Cambridge Elements

Elements in Phonetics
edited by
David Deterding
Universiti Brunei Darussalam

THE PHONETICS OF TAIWANESE

Janice Fon
National Taiwan University

Hui-lu Khoo
National Taiwan Normal University

CAMBRIDGE UNIVERSITY PRESS

Shaftesbury Road, Cambridge CB2 8EA, United Kingdom

One Liberty Plaza, 20th Floor, New York, NY 10006, USA

477 Williamstown Road, Port Melbourne, VIC 3207, Australia

314–321, 3rd Floor, Plot 3, Splendor Forum, Jasola District Centre,
New Delhi – 110025, India

103 Penang Road, #05–06/07, Visioncrest Commercial, Singapore 238467

Cambridge University Press is part of Cambridge University Press & Assessment,
a department of the University of Cambridge.

We share the University's mission to contribute to society through the pursuit of
education, learning and research at the highest international levels of excellence.

www.cambridge.org
Information on this title: www.cambridge.org/9781009566803

DOI: 10.1017/9781009566834

When citing this work, please include a reference to the DOI 10.1017/9781009566834

First published 2024

A catalogue record for this publication is available from the British Library.

ISBN 978-1-009-56680-3 Hardback
ISBN 978-1-009-56682-7 Paperback
ISSN 2634-1689 (online)
ISSN 2634-1670 (print)

Additional resources for this publication at www.cambridge.org/Fon

The Phonetics of Taiwanese

Elements in Phonetics

DOI: 10.1017/9781009566834
First published online: December 2024

Janice Fon
National Taiwan University

Hui-lu Khoo
National Taiwan Normal University

Author for correspondence: Janice Fon, jfon@ntu.edu.tw

Abstract: Taiwanese, formerly the lingua franca of Taiwan and currently the second largest language on the island, is genealogically related to Min from the Sino-Tibetan family. Throughout history, it has been influenced by many languages, but only Mandarin has exerted heavy influences on its phonological system. This Element provides an overview of the sound inventory in mainstream Taiwanese and details its major dialectal differences. In addition, the Element introduces speech materials that could be used for studying the phonetics of Taiwanese, including datasets from both read and spontaneous speech. Based on the data, this Element provides an analysis of Taiwanese phonetics, covering phenomena in consonants, vowels, tones, syllables, and prosody. Some of the results are in line with previous studies, while others imply potential new directions in which the language might be analyzed and might evolve. The Element ends with suggestions for future research lines for the phonetics of the language.

Keywords: Taiwanese phonetics, Taiwanese tone sandhi circle, Taiwanese dialectal variation, Taiwanese–Mandarin interaction, Taiwanese neutralization

ISBNs: 9781009566803 (HB), 9781009566827 (PB), 9781009566834 (OC)
ISSNs: 2634-1689 (online), 2634-1670 (print)

Contents

1 Introduction   1

2 Existing Research   6

3 Dialectal Variations in Taiwanese   27

4 Materials for Research on Taiwanese   33

5 Acoustic Analysis of the Pronunciation of Taiwanese   36

6 Future Research   61

   Appendix   62

   References   73

1 Introduction

Taiwanese, also known as Taiwan Southern Min or Taiwanese Hokkien, is a language spoken in Taiwan, a small yet densely populated island off the southeast coast of China (Figure 1). It had been the lingua franca of the island until 1945, when the government mandated Mandarin as the official language (Lin, 2021). Currently, it is still the second most widely spoken language on the island, and about 70 percent of the population have at least some passive knowledge of the language (Huang, 1993).

Taiwanese is genealogically related to Min, a Sino-Tibetan language spoken in Fujian province on the southeast coast of China (Lin, 2001). During the seventeenth century, population pressure initiated a prolonged wave of migration of Min speakers from Fujian to Taiwan. As the influx continued into the eighteenth century, Min speakers eventually outnumbered the indigenous Austronesian speakers of the island and became the majority of the population. The diaspora originated mainly from two cities in Fujian, Tsiangtsiu and Tsuantsiu. The Min dialects spoken at these two places differ slightly in their sound inventories and phonological rules, but are in general mutually intelligible. They became the main ingredients for the later formation of Taiwanese.

During the early stage of immigration, the two dialects were kept relatively distinct, as the original immigrants tended to cluster amongst their kin. However, in time, dialectal mixing and merging became unavoidable due to frequent contacts between the two varieties. Language contact with Hakka (also a Chinese immigrant language), Pepohoan (Austronesian languages of the plain indigenous tribes), Dutch (during Dutch colonial rule 1624–62 and 1664–8), and Japanese (during Japanese colonial rule 1895–1945) also brought in a large number of lexical items, eventually resulting in a new language we now call Taiwanese (Lin, 2001). In fact, the first mention of the term *Taiwanese* probably appeared during the Japanese colonial era. In his *A Composite Japanese-Taiwanese Dictionary* (Ogawa, 1907) and *A Composite Taiwanese-Japanese Dictionary* (Ogawa, 1931, 1932), Ogawa referred to the language as *Taiuango*, which means Taiwanese in Japanese. The first ever textbooks on Taiwanese were probably also created during this time in order to equip Japanese civil servants and police officers with an adequate level of language proficiency with which to interact smoothly with local residents (Ichikawa, 2013).

Mixing between the Tsiangtsiu and Tsuantsiu dialects was not homogeneous across Taiwan. Some had more traits of one while others had more of the other. Based on the degree of mixing between the two dialects, Ang (2003) categorized Taiwanese into three major dialects: Pro-Tsiang, which has a greater flavor of the Tsiangtsiu variety; Pro-Tsuan, which has a greater tang of the Tsuantsiu

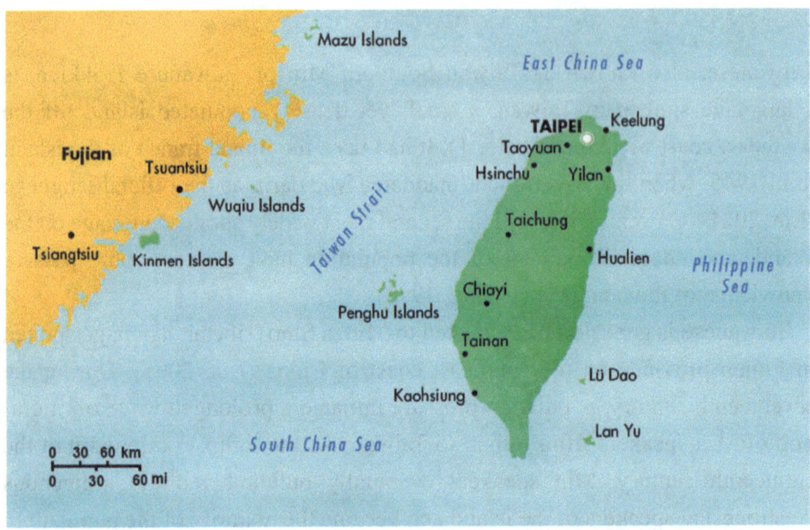

Figure 1 Map of Taiwan marked in green.

variety; and Mix, which incorporates both varieties in a more balanced fashion, although it still leans slightly toward the Tsiangtsiu variety. Figure 2 shows the approximate distributions of the three dialects. The Pro-Tsuan dialect is mainly spoken in the north and on the west coast of central Taiwan, while the Pro-Tsiang dialect mainly appears along the north coast and in central Taiwan. Finally, the Mix dialect is prevalent in the southern part of Taiwan. Because proportionately more speakers have adopted Taiwanese as their primary language in southern Taiwan (Table 1) (National Statistics ROC, 2021), the Mix dialect is currently the most dominant variety (Ang, 1992) and is recognized as the mainstream accent of Taiwanese (Ministry of Education ROC, 2020). Notice that this mainstream variety is not yet completely homogeneous. Regional subdialects still exist in the middle- and old-aged generations, while the younger generation shows more accent merging (Hsu 2015, 2016). Nevertheless, it is currently a widely recognized variety by Taiwanese speakers and is adopted in dictionaries published by the government (Ministry of Education ROC, 2020).

Throughout history, Taiwanese has encountered two government-mandated language promotion movements that threatened its status as a lingua franca. The first one was during the Japanese colonial time. During the early stage of Japanese rule, the Japanese language was promoted but not to the exclusion of local languages. However, between 1937 and 1945, a stricter Japanization policy (the Kōminka Movement) was implemented (Chou, 1996; Lin, 2001). Taiwanese newspapers and schools were banned, and the use of Taiwanese was

Table 1 Min usage calculated by the percentage of speakers using the language as the primary or the secondary means of daily communication in different regions of Taiwan.

%	Northern	Central	Southern	Eastern
Primary	18.17	41.40	48.42	18.57
Secondary	61.43	49.52	46.23	47.43

Adapted from the 2020 Population and Housing Census conducted by the National Statistics ROC (2021)

Figure 2 Distribution of the three major Taiwanese dialects.

forbidden in public institutions. Families were awarded the honorable title of *Kokugo Katei* or *Kokugo no Ie* ('national language family') when they could demonstrate that all members conversed only in Japanese at home. Such families were granted better opportunities in education, career development, and business permit approval (Wu, 2000). Despite all this, Taiwanese demonstrated resilience to the challenges. By 1943, although at least 80 percent of the population could speak Japanese at a fluency level of a sixth grader or above, less than 1.3 percent of the households were granted *Kokugo Katei* (Chou, 1996). In other words, Taiwanese speakers became fluent in everyday Japanese, and educated people were literate in Japanese writing, but their mother tongue and daily language remained largely Taiwanese.

The second language promotion movement was the Mandarin-only policy implemented after the retrocession of Taiwan from Japan to the Republic of China in 1945 at the end of World War II (Huang, 1993; Lin, 2001). In a rush to consolidate power, the new government instigated strict measures to promote Mandarin. The use of Taiwanese was banned from schools and public domains. Poor Mandarin ability was considered a school misconduct and the use of Taiwanese was seriously punished. Broadcasting companies were strictly regulated and highly censored with regard to the proportion of Taiwanese programs. Successful applications to government and teaching positions depended heavily on the Mandarin proficiency of the applicants, as Taiwanese and all the other non-Mandarin languages were demoted to vernaculars and were thought unfit for formal occasions and respectable job positions. In other words, Taiwan had become a strictly diglossic society. Mandarin was the exclusive high language and Taiwanese, despite being the native language of more than 70 percent of the population (Huang, 1993), could merely function as a low language. The Mandarin-only policy ended officially in 1987, when martial law was lifted.

Although on the surface Taiwanese also seemed to have survived the second language promotion movement, its vitality has been in serious decline (Chen, 2010a). According to National Statistics ROC (2021), there is a positive correlation between speaker age and the likelihood of acquiring Taiwanese as one's first language (Table 2). For people aged fifty-five and older, 75 percent acquired Taiwanese first. However, for youngsters aged fourteen and younger, only 22 percent did the same, and 76 percent acquired Mandarin first instead. The adoption of Taiwanese as one's primary language also shows the same trend. For people aged beyond sixty-five, more than 65 percent adopted Taiwanese as their primary language, while for those aged under forty-five, only 15 percent did so, and close to 85 percent adopted Mandarin as their everyday language instead. More important, within each age group, the percentage for acquiring Taiwanese first is always higher than that for adopting it as

Table 2 Percentages of Taiwanese and Mandarin first acquired in childhood and used as the primary language across different age groups.

Age range	First acquired		Primary language	
	Taiwanese	**Mandarin**	**Taiwanese**	**Mandarin**
6–14	22	76	7	92
15–24	30	67	11	89
25–34	38	58	15	84
35–44	51	43	22	77
45–54	62	30	32	67
55–64	70	21	49	48
65 and older	75	14	66	28

Adapted from the 2020 Population and Housing Census conducted by the National Statistics ROC (2021)

the primary language. This bleakly suggests that Taiwanese is quickly losing ground. Even though the government did not officially ban the use of Taiwanese in private domains during the Mandarin-only Movement, people have spontaneously refrained from using the language in their everyday lives, possibly due to self-censorship (Chen, 2010a; Yap, 2018). This creates a large intergenerational transmission gap for Taiwanese language and culture. Nowadays, it is not uncommon to observe grandparents struggling to utter Mandarin words in order to communicate with their grandchildren, even in southern parts of Taiwan where Taiwanese is in fact prevalent (see Table 1). As a consequence, Taiwanese not only lost its status of lingua franca in this second battle, but its survival is seriously jeopardized. Boundaries between Taiwanese dialects have thus been increasingly blurred among the younger generation due to the loss of speakers and decline in speaker proficiency.

Since the 1990s, the government has initiated a series of reversing language shift movements to right the wrongs. Bans on the use of Taiwanese, Hakka, and other indigenous languages in public domains were lifted, and language courses were designed and taught in schools to familiarize students with what should have been their mother tongues (Chen, 1998). Several government-led projects on standardization of written Taiwanese have also been implemented to increase literacy. *Tai-lo*, a romanization alphabet designed for Taiwanese, was created by merging earlier major systems (Ministry of Education ROC, 2008). Assignment criteria for Taiwanese sinographs were also established for high-frequency words to eliminate idiosyncratic usages (Ministry of Education ROC, 2014). Finally, an online Taiwanese dictionary was compiled to facilitate language learning and use (Ministry of Education ROC, 2020). Research on

Taiwanese began to gain popularity (Khoo, 2019). In 2018, the Taiwan Congress passed the Development of National Languages Act, officially granting all languages spoken in Taiwan an equal legal status (Ministry of Culture ROC, 2019).

This Element intends to provide an overview on the phonetics of Taiwanese. Section 2 provides a review of major previous literature on the consonants, vowels, tones, syllables, and prosody of the standard dialect of Taiwanese. Section 3 focuses on some major dialectal variations still robust in the society. Section 4 introduces two research materials, one read and the other spontaneous, for interested researchers to have quick access to actual Taiwanese data, and Section 5 utilizes these materials to provide acoustic measurements for some of the phenomena mentioned in previous literature. Finally, in Section 6, we propose future research directions in Taiwanese worth exploring.

Revitalizing a language already on the decline is truly a mammoth undertaking, and we are all aware of the numerous obstacles ahead. However, it is not without hope. According to a large survey ($N = 2,139$) in Chen (2010a), more than 70 percent of the interviewees agreed that Taiwanese is a marker of solidarity and is worth preserving. As we currently still have enough fluent speakers in the language community, it is possible to provide an enriched environment for both our beginning and advanced learners to develop a fully functional language system of Taiwanese (Hsu, 2018). It merely requires all of us to pitch in and patiently wait for the moment to enjoy the fruits of our toil.

2 Existing Research

This section introduces the consonants, vowels, tones, syllable structure, and prosody of mainstream Taiwanese.

2.1 Consonants

Mainstream Taiwanese has eighteen consonants (Chang, 1989). It has a large set of noncontinuants, including nine plosives, three nasals, and three affricates, and only three continuants, including two fricatives and one approximant (Table 3). In the following, we will look at the phonological patterning of each sound category in turn.

2.1.1 Voiced Stops, Nasal Stops, and /l/

Aside from the missing /d/, Taiwanese has a very balanced set of oral stops, including the voiceless unaspirated /p t k/, the voiceless aspirated /pʰ tʰ kʰ/, and the voiced /b g/ (Chang, 1989). The nasal stops /m n ŋ/ also parallel neatly along the three places of articulation. In the literature, however, there has been

Table 3 Consonants of mainstream Taiwanese.

	Bilabial	**Dental**	**Velar**	**Glottal**
Plosive	p pʰ b	t tʰ	k kʰ g	ʔ
Nasal	m	n	ŋ	
Affricate		ts tsʰ dz		
Fricative		s		h
Approximant		l		

Table 4 Examples of the complementary distribution of /b l g/ and /m n ŋ/. Superscript numbers after IPA transcriptions indicate tone numbers.

Tai-lo	**IPA**	**Gloss**	**Tai-lo**	**IPA**	**Gloss**
bā	[ba⁷]	'to fit'	*mā*	[mã⁷]	'to scold'
lî	[li⁵]	'to leave'	*nî*	[nĩ⁵]	'year'
gōo	[gɔ⁷]	'five'	*ngōo*	[ŋɔ̃⁷]	'to realize'

Superscript numbers indicate tones.

a long-standing tradition to include /l/ as part of the voiced stop series to stand in place of what should have been a /d/ (Chung, 1996; Lin, 2001). Although some have argued that there is some phonetic basis to this and have claimed that Taiwanese /l/ has a stop-like quality (Chang, 1989), the motivation is really phonological.

In Taiwanese, a phonological rule dictates that the nasality of a voiced stop onset and its following vowel has to be consistent. Voiced oral stops are followed by oral vowels, while nasal stops are followed by nasal vowels (Chang, 1989; Chung, 1996; Lin, 2001). For the bilabial and velar positions, this indicates that [b g] are in complementary distribution with their homorganic nasals [m ŋ]. For the dental position, since /d/ is missing, the system picks the next closest candidate possible, and the alternation occurs between [l] and [n]. The rule could be summarized as (1). Table 4 shows some examples.[1]

(1)   /b l g /→[m n ŋ]/$_Ṽ

---

[1] Notice that the Tai-lo romanization system is to a large extent IPA-based. There are only four minor deviations for consonants for easier typesetting. The superscript /h/ for the voiceless aspirated stops /pʰ tʰ kʰ/ becomes non-superscript in *ph*, *th*, and *kh*, as in *phuē* /pʰue/ 'blanket'; the glottal stop /ʔ/ becomes h, as in *m̄-koh* /m̩.kɔʔ/ 'but'; the velar nasal /ŋ/ becomes *ng*, as in *hó-khang* /hɔ.kʰaŋ/ 'good opportunity'; finally, the voiced dental affricate /dz/ becomes *j*, as in *jiân-āu* /dzian.au̯/ 'then'. For a detailed description, please see the Ministry of Education's manual (Ministry of Education ROC, 2008).

A controversy related to the rule in (1) is the phonemic status of the onsets [b l g] and [m n ŋ]. Since the two sets of sounds are in complementary distribution, some researchers followed the classical analysis and considered them as allophones of the same phonemes. [m n ŋ] are thus deemed as mere allophonic realizations of /b l g/ before nasalized vowels, and do not have a phonemic status of their own (Chang, 1989; Lin, 2001; Tung, 1968). However, other scholars viewed the distribution as an accidental gap and regarded the two sets of sounds as separate phonemes (Cheng & Cheng, 1987; Ting, 1985). Experimental data supported the first view more. Pan (2004) found that listeners tended to ignore the phonetic differences between onsets [b] and [m] and categorize them as the same phoneme. Wang (1996) also showed that both the [b m] pair and the [g ŋ] pair were accepted as allophones of the same phonemes in the onset position. However, similar results were not observed for the [l n] pair. This implies that even though /l/ takes the place of the missing /d/ in Rule (1), it likely has a phonemic status apart from /n/, unlike the [b m] and [g ŋ] pairs. Therefore, the phonemic transcription of *mā* 'to scold' and *ngōo* 'to realize' in Table 4 should probably be /bã/ and /gɔ̃/, respectively, while that of *nî* 'year' should still be /nĩ/. However, this does not mean that Taiwanese lacks /m ŋ/ in its phoneme inventory. Both can act as syllabic nasals as in *m̄-koh* /m̩.kə/ 'but' and *n̂g-sik* / ŋ̩.sik/ 'yellow', and are allowed in the coda position like /n/, as in *kâm* /kam/ 'to hold in mouth' and *kâng* /kaŋ/ 'same', and are thus still regarded as phonemes.

2.1.2 Sibilant Realization

Taiwanese has four sibilants in total, including one fricative /s/ and three affricates /ts tsʰ dz/. Of the four, the voiced affricate is the most variable and has several allophones. Besides the canonical [dz], there are also two free variants, [z] and [l], as shown in (2) (Ang, 1997, 2003; Chen, 1995; Lin, 1995). The developmental process is construed to be from [dz] to [z] to [l], and is deemed to be motivated by ease of articulation (Chuang & Fon, 2017a, 2018). Voiced affricates are composed of a voiced stop and a voiced fricative, both of which are physiologically strenuous (Ohala, 1983). Voiced stops require low intraoral pressure relative to the subglottal pressure to maintain voicing. However, when the closure is long, the transglottal pressure difference can drop quickly, and voicing ceases. Voiced fricatives are even more difficult. Besides the transglottal pressure difference required for voicing, the intraoral pressure also has to be higher than the atmospheric pressure to maintain high air velocity. When the air velocity is too low, frication noise cannot be created, and the result is an approximant, such as [l] (Ohala, 1983). Therefore, the development of [dz]→[z]→[l] is considered a weakening process with an articulatory basis.

(2)   /dz/ → [dz z l] (free variation)

There is an additional variant [g] for /dz/, which only occurs before /i/, as shown in (3). This variant is generally believed to be influenced by Hakka through language contact (Ang, 2003, 2012). Speakers are not homogeneous with regard to how they treat this variant. Some use it in free variation (Chen, 1995), while others use it in complementary distribution with [dz], [z], and [l] (Lin, 1995).

(3)   /(d)z/ → [g] / $__ i

All four of the sibilants undergo an assimilation rule of palatalization when preceding /i/, as shown in (4). Since /dz/ has two free variants that are sibilants (i.e., [dz] and [z]), its palatalized form also has two free variants, [dʑ] and [ʑ] (Ang, 1997, 2003; Chen, 1995; Lin, 1995).

(4)   /s ts tsʰ (d)z/→[ɕ tɕ tɕʰ (d)ʑ] / $__ i

2.2 Vowels

Mainstream Taiwanese has six oral monophthongs /i e a ɔ u ə/ and four nasal monophthongs /ĩ ẽ ã ɔ̃/ (Figure 3) (Chang, 1989). If only oral vowels are considered, it is deemed a symmetric six-vowel system and is assumed to be relatively stable (Chen, 2010b). Table 5 shows some examples.[2] In addition to the monophthongs, Taiwanese also allows eight diphthongs, including five rising diphthongs /i̯a i̯ə u̯a u̯e u̯i/, and three falling diphthongs /ai̯ au̯ iu̯/. The nonsyllabic vowel targets are always /i̯/ or /u̯/, but the syllabic vowel targets are somewhat different between the rising and falling diphthongs. For the

Table 5 Examples of oral and nasal monophthongs.

Oral vowels			Nasalized vowels		
Tai-lo	**IPA**	**Gloss**	**Tai-lo**	**IPA**	**Gloss**
tī	/ti⁷/	'chopsticks'	*tīnn*	/tĩ⁷/	'full'
se	/se¹/	'muslin'	*senn*	/sẽ¹/	'to give birth'
ta	/ta¹/	'dry'	*tann*	/tã¹/	'to bear'
kôo	/kɔ⁵/	'to paste'	*kôonn*	/kɔ̃⁵/	'to snore'

---

[2] Vowels in the Tai-lo romanization also follow the IPA system closely. There are only three deviations for vowels for easier typesetting. The /ə/ is represented by *o*, as in *hó-giàh* /hə.gi̯aʔ/ 'rich'; the mid-back vowel /ɔ/ is represented by *oo*, as in *sóo-i* /sɔ.i/ 'so'; finally, nasal vowels are represented by adding *nn* after the vowel, as in *enn-á* /ẽ.a/ 'baby'. Diphthongs and triphthongs are written by juxtaposing the relevant vowel targets together, as in *tsuân-pōo* /tsu̯an.pɔ/ 'all' and *khiau-kha* /kʰi̯au̯.kʰa/ 'to cross one's legs'. Please see the Ministry of Education's manual for a detailed description (Ministry of Education ROC, 2008).

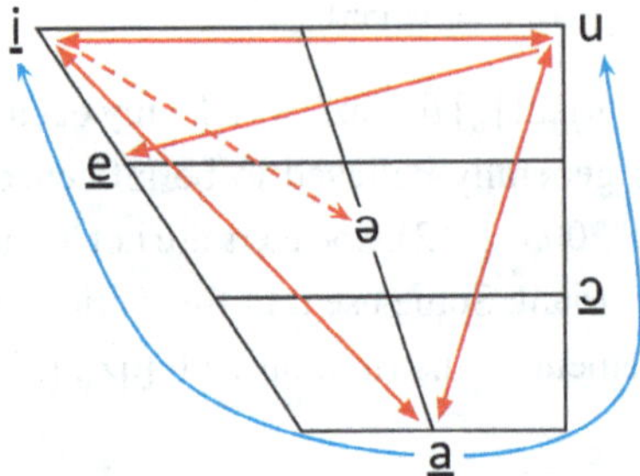

Figure 3 Vowel chart of mainstream Taiwanese. Underlined vowels are those that also have a nasal counterpart. Red arrows indicate diphthongs. The direction of an arrow represents the sequential order of the vowel targets, and double arrows indicate that both orders are allowed. The blue double arrow indicates the two triphthongs. Arrows with solid lines are diphthongs and triphthongs that also have a nasal counterpart, while the arrow with a dashed line only has the oral version, but not the nasal one.

former, vowels of all three height levels can be used, including /a ə e i/, while for the latter, they are restricted to only /a/ and /i/. Rounded vowels cannot act as the syllabic target regardless of diphthong types. The designation of the syllabic target in /u̯i/ and /iu̯/ is especially interesting. Although both are composed of the two high vowel targets /i/ and /u/, Hsu (2004) argued that /i/ has higher sonority than /u/ using rhyming patterns and acoustic measurements as evidence, and designated /i/ as the syllabic target for both. Of the eight diphthongs, seven are with a nasal counterpart, including four of the rising diphthongs /ĩ̯ã ũ̯ã ũ̯ĩ ũ̯ẽ/, and all three of the falling diphthongs /ãĩ̯ ãũ̯ ĩũ̯/. Taiwanese also has two triphthongs, /i̯au̯/ and /u̯ai̯/, with the syllabic vowel being always /a/. Both of them have a nasal counterpart. Some examples are given in Table 6.

2.3 Tones

Being a tonal language, Taiwanese is rich in tones, and it has an extensive set of tone sandhi rules. It also uses tones to distinguish between stressed and unstressed syllables. In the following, tonal categories and their corresponding rules regarding tone sandhi and stress are introduced.

2.3.1 Tonal Categories

There are in total seven tones in Taiwanese and almost all syllables in Taiwanese are realized with a particular tone (Chang, 1989; Lin, 2001).

Table 6 Examples of oral and nasal diphthongs and triphthongs.

Oral vowels			Nasalized vowels		
Tai-lo	**IPA**	**Gloss**	**Tai-lo**	**IPA**	**Gloss**
kai	/kai̯^{1}/	'should'	*kainn*	/kãĩ̯^{1}/	'to moan'
háu	/hau̯^{2}/	'to cry'	*hàunnh*	/hãũ̯ʔ^8/	'half-cooked'
iû	/iu̯^{5}/	'oil'	*iûnn*	/ĩũ̯^{5}/	'sheep, goat'
kià	/ki̯a^3/	'to mail'	*kiànn*	/kĩ̯ã^3/	'mirror'
kua	/ku̯a^1/	'song'	*kuann*	/kũ̯ã^1/	'liver'
khui	/kʰu̯i^3/	'breath'	*khuinn-uàh*	/kʰũ̯ĩ^3.u̯aʔ^8/	'happy'
buèh-á	/bu̯eʔ^8.a^2/	'sock'	*muê-á*	/bũ̯ẽ^5.a^2/	'plum'
iau	/i̯au̯^{1}/	'hungry'	*iaunn*	/ĩ̯ãũ̯^{1}/	'peek-a-boo'
kuai	/ku̯ai̯^{1}/	'obedient'	*kuainn*	/kũ̯ãĩ̯^{1}/	'to close'

Taiwanese tones are defined by two factors, pitch contour and syllable structure. Tone 4 and Tone 8 are reserved for checked syllables, which are syllables with obstruent codas /p t k ʔ/. Because the voicing ends abruptly, the duration of these two tones is extremely short. The remaining five tones are called smooth tones and occur in all the nonchecked syllables. These tones are longer, and have more variations in their tonal contours. Table 7 shows the descriptions of these tones using both word labels and Chao's (1968) five-point tonal scale, with 1 being the lowest and 5 being the highest in pitch. Notice that although Taiwanese has seven tones, they are numbered from Tone 1 to Tone 5, and then from Tone 7 to Tone 8. Tone 6 is missing. This is because Taiwanese originally had eight tones, but Tone 6 was merged with Tone 2 in its historical evolution. The absence of the historical Tone 6 and the different tone sandhi behaviors of checked and unchecked tones (discussed later in this Element) suggest that this system of tone description might be revised. Nevertheless, here we will continue to use the traditional system.

Of the five smooth tones, there are two level tones, two falling tones, and one rising tone. The two level tones differ in pitch register; one is high-level (Tone 1) and the other is mid-level (Tone 7).[3] Similarly, the two falling tones also differ in pitch register; one is high-falling (Tone 2) and the other is low-falling (Tone 3). There is some debate regarding the actual contour of Tone 3. Some claim that it is

---

[3] Except for Tone 1 and Tone 4, which do not have any overt markers for tones, tonal values are indicated by using diacritics above vowels in the Tai-lo system (Table 7). Please refer to the Ministry of Education's manual for a detailed description (Ministry of Education ROC, 2008).

Table 7 The seven tones of Taiwanese. Underlined tone values indicate short tones.

Tones	Word labels	Chao's tone values					Examples	
		C_1	Y	T	A	C_2		
Tone 1	high-level	55	44	44	44	55	*kun*	'king'
Tone 2	high-falling	53	53	53	41	51	*kún*	'to boil'
Tone 3	low-falling	21	31	11	21	11	*kùn*	'rod'
Tone 4	mid-short	21	32	32	32	3	*kut*	'bone'
Tone 5	mid-rising	24	13	24	23	13	*kûn*	'group'
Tone 7	mid-level	33	33	33	33	33	*kūn*	'county'
Tone 8	high-short	53	33	4	4	5	*kut*	'slippery'

C_1: Chang (1989); Y: Yang (1991); T: Tung (1996); A: Ang (1997); C_2: Chang (1999)

a falling tone (Ang, 1997; Chang, 1989; Yang, 1991), while others argue that it is a low-level tone (Chang, 1999; Tung, 1996). One suspects that this is due to the limits of methodology. Since all of the researchers in Table 7 utilized only subjective judgments but not acoustic measurements in determining tonal values, and since listeners' perceptual acuity is positively correlated with pitch height (Jongman et al., 2017), it is possible that the pitch movements of Tone 3 occur at a pitch register that is too low to be reliably detected. However, since three of the five researchers heard a falling contour, and since acoustic studies also showed a falling contour (Hong & Chan, 2022), Tone 3 is labeled as a low-falling tone in this Element.

As for the two checked tones, although there is large variability among the five researchers with regard to tonal values, especially for Tone 8, at least all of them are unanimous with regard to the relative tonal register. Tone 8 is slightly higher than Tone 4. As for the tonal contour, it seems that Tone 4 is slightly falling, while Tone 8 is more varied. It seems to be either a level or a falling tone. This also coincides with previous acoustic studies (Hong & Chan, 2022). However, since the two tones are rather short in duration, one suspects that the exact tonal contour does not play an important role in tonal perception due to perceptual limits (cf. Jongman et al., 2017). Tonal perception thus likely places more weight on the tonal register instead. Also, although Tone 3 and Tone 4 seem to have very similar tonal contours for most analyses based on Table 7, they are actually perceptually rather distinct, as the two are very different in tonal duration, with the former almost twice as long as the latter (Hong & Chan, 2022).

2.3.2 Tone Sandhi

The aforementioned tones are usually called base tones or citation tones. Taiwanese also has a fairly extensive set of sandhi tone rules that apply to all tonal categories. In a tone sandhi group (TSG), only the last stressed syllable is exempt and receives the base tone. All the preceding syllables undergo the tone sandhi rules and are realized with corresponding sandhi tones, which are phonologically and phonetically different from their base tone counterparts (Chang, 1989; Lin, 2001). A TSG does not have a definite length, and its scope is jointly determined by morphology, syntax, and prosody. For example, when *Tâi-uân* 'Taiwan' and *gín-á* 'child', each of which is a TSG, are compounded together to form *Tâi-uân gín-á* 'native Taiwanese (lit. children of Taiwan)', a larger TSG is formed and only the last syllable *á* is realized in its citation form. The three preceding syllables of *tâi*, *uân*, and *gín* are realized in their sandhi forms. The rule for sandhi tones is summarized in (5).

(5) $T_{base} \rightarrow T_{sandhi} / \underline{\hspace{2em}} + \sigma_1 + \sigma_2 + \ldots + \acute{\sigma}_n]_{TSG}$

Figure 4 shows the tone sandhi circle of mainstream Taiwanese. The five smooth tones go around in a circle when linked by their tone sandhi rules (hence the tone sandhi circle). Except for Tone 5, which can only occur as a citation form but not a sandhi form, all the remaining four tones can act as both. For example, when a high-level tonal contour is encountered, there are two reasonable possibilities. It can either be a Tone 1 in its citation form or a Tone 2 in its sandhi form. Only the positioning of the tone could help differentiate between the two. For the mid-level tonal contour, it could be even more complicated, as there are then three possibilities. It can be a Tone 7 in its citation form, or a Tone 1 in its sandhi form, or a Tone 5 in its sandhi form. For a word like *pîng-an* 'peace', which is composed of a /piŋ/ syllable in Tone 5

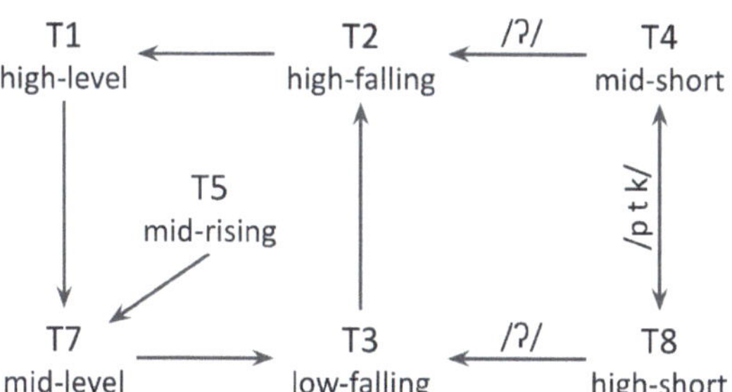

Figure 4 The tone sandhi circle of mainstream Taiwanese tones.
The direction of the arrows indicates the tonal change required by the sandhi rules when a citation tone is changed to its sandhi tone. T: tone.

Table 8 Examples of the regular tone sandhi rules.

Tai-lo	Sandhi form	Gloss
tang-pîng	/taŋ^1.piŋ^5/→[taŋ^7.piŋ^5]	'east'
báng-thâng	/baŋ^2.tʰaŋ^5/→[baŋ^1.tʰaŋ^5]	'bugs'
tàng-sng	/taŋ^3.sŋ^1/→[taŋ^2.sŋ^1]	'stingy'
kak-tōo	/kak^4.tɔ^7/→[kak^8.tɔ^7]	'angle'
kah-ì	/kaʔ^4.i^3/→[ka^2.i^3]	'like'
tâng-o	/taŋ^5.ə^1/→[taŋ^7.ə^1]	'crown daisy'
kāng-khuán	/kaŋ^7.kʰuan^2/→[kaŋ^3.kʰuan^2]	'same'
ga̍k-khì	/gak^8.kʰi^3/→[gak^4.kʰi^3]	'musical instrument'
tsia̍h-pn̄g	/tsiaʔ^8.pŋ^7/→[tsia^3.pŋ^7]	'eat'

and an /an/ syllable in Tone 1, it is pronounced as a /piŋ/ in Tone 7 plus an /an/ in Tone 1 when the two syllables are strung together (Table 8).

Tone sandhi of the two checked tones follows a different set of rules, and is coda-dependent. For syllables ending with /p t k/, Tone 4 and Tone 8 act as the sandhi tone for each other (Figure 4) (Chang, 1989; Cheng, 1973; Lin, 2001). For example, *kak-tōo* /kak^4.tɔ^7/ 'angle' is realized as [kak^8.tɔ^7], and *ga̍k-khì* / gak^8.kʰi^3/ 'musical instrument' is realized as [gak^4.kʰi^3] (Table 8). However, this does not necessarily entail that the phonetic realization of a sandhi Tone 4 is identical to that of a citation Tone 8, or vice versa. Instead, it merely specifies the fact that the sandhi Tone 4 is a high short tone while the sandhi Tone 8 is a low short tone.

There is a different set of sandhi rules regarding checked tones ending with /ʔ/ (Figure 4) (Chang, 1989; Cheng, 1973; Lin, 2001). This is probably because there is an additional coda-dropping rule for /ʔ/ prior to the sandhi rules when the syllable is in a TSG-internal position, as shown in (6). With the final obstruent gone, the syllable now becomes lengthened, and what was originally the pitch excursion for Tone 4 and Tone 8 is now phonetically respectively closer to a low-falling Tone 3 and a mid-level Tone 7 instead. Therefore, they follow the rules for Tone 3 and Tone 7 and their sandhi forms become high-falling Tone 2 and low-falling Tone 3, respectively (Figure 4). Please see Table 8 for some examples.

(6)   /ʔ/ → ∅ / ____ + σ$_1$ + σ$_2$ + ... + σ$_n$]$_{TSG}$

2.3.3 Exceptions to Regular Tone Sandhi Rules

There are three groups of words that are exceptions to the aforementioned tone sandhi rules (Lu, 2003). All of them abide by rules that are somewhat different from the default sandhi rules. The first group involves some high-frequency words, such as *khì* 'go' and *kah* 'and'. Instead of the sandhi rules applying once, they apply twice. For example, *khì tó* /k^{h}i^3.tə^2/ 'where do you want to go? (lit. go where)' should have been realized as *[k^{h}i^2 tə^2] according to the sandhi rules (Figure 4). However, the actual realization is in fact [k^{h}i^1 tə^2] instead. Similarly, *guá kah lí* /gua^2 ka$ʔ^4$ li^2/ 'me and you' should have been *[gua^1 ka^2 li^2], but is instead realized as [gua^1 ka^1 li^2].

The second group of exceptions involves the diminutive suffix *-á*. More than half of the tones abide by a different set of sandhi rules when followed by the suffix, including Tone 3, Tone 7, /ʔ/-ending Tone 4, and /ʔ/-ending Tone 8 (Table 9). Tone 3 and Tone 4 have Tone 1 as their sandhi tone by applying the sandhi rules twice. Tone 8 has Tone 7 as its sandhi tone by applying the sandhi rule once and then reversing the sandhi rule after [ʔ] deletion. For example, *thòo-á* /t^{h}ɔ^3.a^2/ 'rabbit' should have been *[t^{h}ɔ^2.a^2], but is realized as [t^{h}ɔ^1.a^2] instead. Similarly, *hiòh-á* /hiə$ʔ^8$.a^2/ 'leaf' should have been *[hiə^3.a^2], but is realized as [hiə^7.a^2] instead. Tone 7 is the oddball in this set, as it does not undergo the tone sandhi rules at all. For example, *phōo-á* /p^{h}ɔ^7.a^2/ 'booklet' should have been *[p^{h}ɔ^3.a^2], but it remains [p^{h}ɔ^7.a^2] instead. One suspects that the motivation for these exceptions might be avoidance of low-ending tones. Since *-á* begins high, preventing the previous tone from ending low might make it easier for tonal articulation.

Table 9 Examples of the exception tone sandhi rules before the diminutive marker *-á*. Boldface indicates deviations from regular sandhi rules.

Tai-lo	Before *-á*	Gloss
kim-á	/kim^1.a^2/→[kim^7.a^2]	'gold'
láng-á	/laŋ^2.a^2/→[laŋ^1.a^2]	'cage'
thòo-á	/t^{h}ɔ^3.a^2/→[t^{h}ɔ^1.a^2]	**'rabbit'**
tik-á	/tik^4.a^2/→[tik^8.a^2]	'bamboo'
ah-á	/a$ʔ^4$.a^2/→[a^1.a^2]	**'duck'**
iûnn-á	/ĩũ^5.a^2/→[ĩũ^7.a^2]	'sheep, goat'
phōo-á	/p^{h}ɔ^7.a^2/→[p^{h}ɔ^7.a^2]	**'booklet'**
tsha̍t-á	/tsh^{h}at^8.a^2/→[tsh^{h}at^4.a^2]	'thief'
hiòh-á	/hiə$ʔ^8$.a^2/→[hiə^7.a^2]	**'leaf'**

Finally, the third group of exceptions involves a morphological structure specific to adjectives. In Taiwanese, triple reduplication is adopted for emphasis (Chang, 1989; Lin, 2001). For example, while *âng* means *red*, *âng-âng-âng* means *extremely red*. Special sandhi rules are applied to the first syllable of these structures for four of the tones, including Tone 1, Tone 5, Tone 7, and Tone 8, so that it becomes a Tone 5 (Table 10). The second and the third syllables follow the regular sandhi rules. For instance, when *kim* /kim^1/ 'shiny' is triply reduplicated, it becomes [kim^5.kim^7.kim^1], not *[kim^7.kim^7.kim^1]. Notice that for Tone 8, the exception sandhi rule would result in a checked syllable being paired with a smooth tone – for example, *bat* /bat^8/ 'fitting tightly' becomes [bat^5.bat^4.bat^8]. The first syllable is realized as a mid-rising Tone 5 without deleting the final /t/. However, since the first syllable of triply reduplicated adjectives is always lengthened, the checked Tone 8 is lengthened accordingly and would not have trouble realizing the smooth tone fully.

2.3.4 Tone versus Stress

Besides a complicated tonal system, Taiwanese also has stress, and its stress is realized largely through tone (Lu, 2003). All stressed syllables in Taiwanese receive a tone, either a base tone or a sandhi tone. On the other hand, unstressed syllables are not assigned any tone and are intrinsically short. Based on how their pitch register is realized, unstressed syllables can be of two types. The first adopts the pitch register of the end of the preceding syllable. The nominalization marker --*ê* and the aspect marker --*ah* are of this type.[4] The second type consistently assumes a low falling contour, much like that of a Tone 3 or Tone 4, regardless of the preceding tonal

Table 10 Examples of the exception tone sandhi rules in triply reduplicated adjectives. Boldface indicates deviations from regular rules.

Tai-lo	Triple reduplication	Gloss
kim	**/kim^1.kim^1.kim^1/→[kim^5.kim^7.kim^1]**	**'shiny'**
tsún	/tsun^2.tsun^2.tsun^2/→[tsun^1.tsun^1.tsun^2]	'accurate'
tàng	/taŋ^3.taŋ^3.taŋ^3/→[taŋ^2.taŋ^2.taŋ^3]	'freezing'
kip	/kip^4.kip^4.kip^4/→[kip^8.kip^8.kip^4]	'rushed'
khuah	/kʰua$ʔ^4$.kʰua$ʔ^4$.kʰua$ʔ^4$/→[kʰua^2.kʰua^2.kʰua$ʔ^4$]	'spatious'
tâm	**/tam^5.tam^5.tam^5/→[tam^5.tam^7.tam^5]**	**'wet'**
tīng	**/tiŋ^7.tiŋ^7.tiŋ^7/→[tiŋ^5.tiŋ^3.tiŋ^7]**	**'hard'**
bat	**/bat^8.bat^8.bat^8/→[bat^5.bat^4.bat^8]**	**'fitting tightly'**
peh	**/pe$ʔ^8$.pe$ʔ^8$.pe$ʔ^8$/→[pe^5.pe^3.pe$ʔ^8$]**	**'white'**

---

[4] Unstressed syllables are preceded by double dashes in the Tai-lo system (Ministry of Education ROC, 2008).

Table 11 Examples of the exception tone sandhi rules regarding unstressed syllables. Superscript H and L represent the pitch height of the unstressed syllable. Unstressed syllables above the dotted line belong to the first type, while those below belong to the second (see text).

Tai-lo	Before unstressed syllable	Gloss
sio--ê	/sio^1.e^5/→[sio^1.e^H]	'things that are hot'
líng--ê	/liŋ^2.e^5/→[liŋ^2.e^L]	'things that are cold'
lim--ah	/lim^1.aʔ^4/→[lim^1.aʔ^H]	'have drunk'
khùn--ah	/kʰun^3.aʔ^4/→[kʰun^3.aʔ^L]	'have slept'
tsim--tiȯh	/tsim^1.ti̯ə ʔ^8/→[tsim^1.ti̯ə ʔ^L]	'have kissed'
khuànn--tiȯh	/kʰṳ̃ã^3.ti̯ə ʔ^8/→[kʰṳ̃ã^3.ti̯ə ʔ^L]	'have seen'
pue--khí-lâi	/pṳe^1.kʰi^2.lai̯^{5}/→[pṳe^1.kʰi^L.lai̯^{L}]	'take off'
tsáu--khí-lâi	/tsau̯^{2}.kʰi^2.lai̯^{5}/→[tsau̯^{2}.kʰi^L.lai̯^{L}]	'start to run'

environment. Verbal complements *--tiȯh* and *--khí-lâi* are of this type. Table 11 shows some examples of unstressed syllables. Notice that the syllable preceding an unstressed syllable is always realized in its base tone.

2.4 Syllables

The syllable structure of Taiwanese is of a CGVX skeleton, in which only V is obligatory (Chang, 1989; Cheng & Cheng, 1987; Chung, 1996). It can be filled by a vowel or a syllabic nasal /m̩ ŋ̍/. All consonants except for /ʔ/ can occur in the C slot. The G slot is reserved for the onglide of a rising diphthong – that is, /i̯/ and /u̯/. The final X slot can be filled with an offglide of a falling diphthong, a nasal /m n ŋ/, or an unreleased stop of /p t k ʔ/.

Traditionally, a Taiwanese syllable is composed of an initial and a final (Chappell, 2019; Chung, 1996). The initial is the onset consonant in the C slot, and the final is the rest of the syllable. The final is further divided into the medial and the rhyme. The medial position is reserved for the onglide of a diphthong – that is, the G slot. The rhyme is composed of the nucleus (the V slot) and the coda (the X slot). Figure 5 shows an example.

Syllable boundaries are relatively fluid in Taiwanese and can be modified, weakened, or even erased altogether through phonetic, phonological, morphological, and prosodic rules. In the following, four types of boundary modifications are introduced: coda obstruent deletion is phonetically licensed; anticipatory assimilation is phonetically and phonologically motivated; gemination is morphologically triggered; syllable fusion is largely predicted by prosody. Each of these is discussed in what follows.

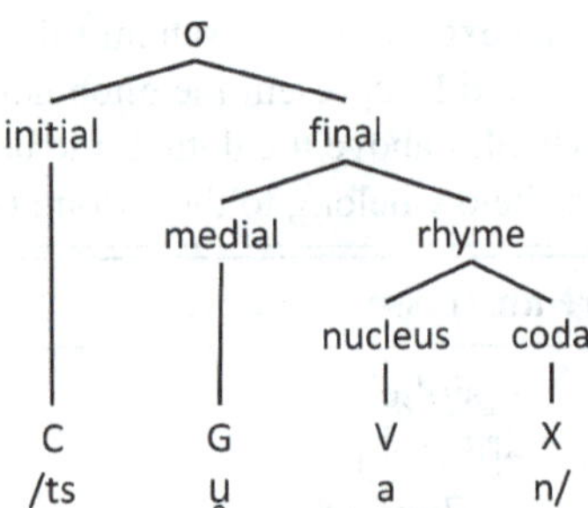

Figure 5 An illustration of the classical view of the subsyllabic organization of a Taiwanese syllable using *tsuân* 'total' as an example.

2.4.1 Deletion of Coda Obstruents

In Section 2.2, we mentioned a rule regarding the deletion of /ʔ/ in TSG-internal positions. However, recent studies have shown that there are more cases of coda deletion than what is prescribed by the phonological rule. In other words, deletion is observed for all coda obstruents /p t k ʔ/, but the rate is especially high for /ʔ/. Using acoustic measurements and electroglottography, Pan (2017) observed that the deletion rate for /ʔ/ is higher than 80 percent, while that for /p t k/ is lower than 15 percent. Similar results were also found in Chen (2009b, 2010b) and Pan and Lyu (2021). /ʔ/ is always more prone to be deleted than /p t k/, and more prone to be deleted in Tone 8 than Tone 4. As /ʔ/ not only has little vowel transition (Chu & Lin, 2010), but also lacks the visual cues commonly found in oral stops, it might be harder for listeners to perceive and is thus more prone to deletion.

2.4.2 Anticipatory Assimilation of Codas

Assimilation in Taiwanese is largely anticipatory, and mainly occurs on coda consonants (Chang, 1989; Lin, 2001). Table 12 shows some examples. It is interesting to note that all lexical items do not apply the rule with the same frequency. For some, such as *sin-pū* 'daughter-in-law', assimilation is obligatory. The underlying form /sin.pu/ is practically never heard. However, for others, such as *sin-bûn* 'news', assimilation is optional, and its application is probably governed by a variety of performance factors, such as speech rate, genre, and personal preferences.

2.4.3 Gemination of Coda Stops

The gemination of coda stops can be triggered by a diminutive suffix -*á* [e.g., *niau-á* 'cat (lit. cat-dim.)'], a nominal suffix --*ê* [e.g., *thâi-ti--ê* 'butcher (lit. kill-pig-nom.)'], or a classifier *ê* [e.g., *gōo ê lâng* 'five people (lit. five-CL-people)'].

Table 12 Examples of anticipatory assimilation of codas. Assimilation for the two examples above the dotted line is obligatory, while for the two examples below, it is optional.

Tai-lo	Assimilation	Gloss
sin-pū	/sin.pu/→[sim.pu]	'daughter-in-law'
kim-nî	/kim.ni/→[kin.ni]	'this year'
pak-tóo	/pak.tɔ/→[pat.tɔ]	'stomach'
sin-bûn	/sin.bun/→[sim.bun]	'news'

Table 13 Examples of coda (nasal) stop gemination.

Tai-lo	Gemination (+voicing)	Gloss
ȧp-á	/ap.a/→[ab.ba]	'box'
kim-á	/kim.a/→[kim.ma]	'gold'
gín-á	/gin.a/→[gin.na]	'child
tsi̍t ê	/tsit.e/→[tsil.le]	'one'
tik--ê	/tik.e/→[tig.ge]	'Tik' (a name)
âng--ê	/aŋ.e/→[aŋ.ŋe]	'something red'

It applies to all coda stops except for the glottal stop /ʔ/ (Chappell, 2019; Chiang, 1992; Lien, 1995; Lin, 2001). The process is straightforward for nasal codas as only gemination is involved. The nasal coda of the first syllable is copied to the onset slot of the following syllable to reach the final output – for example, *kim-á* / kim.a/→[kim.ma] 'gold' (Table 13). The situation is a bit more complicated for the oral stops. In addition to gemination, there is also intervocalic voicing, so *ȧp-á* /ap.a/ 'box' is realized as [ab.ba]. For syllables ending with the coda /t/, such as *tsi̍t ê* /tsit.e/ 'one', intervocalic voicing turns the coda into [l] instead, as there is no /d/ in the Taiwanese sound inventory (Table 3).

2.4.4 Syllable Fusion

Syllable fusion is a rather productive process in Taiwanese (Lin, 2001). Table 14 shows some examples. It is clear from the table that the onset of a fused syllable usually comes from that of the first syllable, while the coda usually comes from that of the second syllable. This is captured by Chung's (1996) "edge-in" rule, in which the first segment of the first syllable and the last segment of the last syllable are selected to be in the final fused form. Selection of the vowel nucleus of the fused form seems somewhat trickier. For *tsit-tsūn* 'now', the vowel of the

Table 14 Examples of syllable fusion. Red indicates influences from the first syllable, and blue indicates influences from the second syllable.

Tai-lo	Syllable fusion	Gloss
tsa-hng	/tsa^1.hŋ^1/→[tsaŋ^5]	'yesterday'
tsit-tsūn	/tsit^4.tsun^7/→[tsin^2]	'now'
sî-tsūn	/si^5.tsun^7/→[sin^7] or [sun^7]	'time'
sàu--lòh-lâi	/sau̯^{3}.lə?^{8}.lai̯^{5}/→[sau̯^{3}.lu̯ai̯]	'to sweep down'
sì tsàp it	/si^3.tsap^8.it^4/→[si̯ap^8.it^4]	'forty-one'

first syllable is chosen, but for *sàu--lòh-lâi* 'to sweep down' and *sì tsàp it* 'forty-one', both vowels are incorporated in the final fused form. For *sî-tsūn* 'time', forms with a vowel from either the first or the second syllable have been attested (Li & Myers, 2005). Chung (1996) stated that the nucleus of the fused syllable is awarded to the vowel of the highest sonority (the "vocoid association" rule), with the ones on the left having a higher priority than those on the right (the "L-R-scanning" rule). The final fused form also has to obey the phonotactic constraints of the language (the "maximality constraint" rule). This could then easily explain the fused forms for *tsa-hng* 'yesterday', *sàu--lòh-lâi* 'to sweep down', and *sì tsàp it* 'forty-one'. However, there are also limitations to the rules. For example, they fail to explain why there are two fused forms for *sî-tsūn* 'time' but only one for *tsit-tsūn* 'now' when the two practically have the same vowel combination.

2.5 Prosody

Grouping and prominence are considered the two pillars in prosody (Pierrehumbert, 1980). The former refers to how words are organized into units of various sizes, while the latter refers to how some words are emphasized over others through highlighting devices. The following introduces the two main elements of prosody in Taiwanese.

2.5.1 Prosodic Grouping

With regard to grouping, Peng and Beckman (2003) detailed three levels of prosodic constituents in their prosodic labeling system of Tone and Break Indices for Taiwanese (TW-ToBI), including the syllable, the TSG, and the intonational phrase (IP). Among the three, the syllable is the lowest level. Although syllable boundaries are largely regulated by phonotactics, they are not at all unbreakable. In addition to resyllabification due to affixation (see Section 2.4.3), syllable fusion caused by juncture weakening is often observed in spontaneous speech (see Section 2.4.4), as is illustrated in (7). The bisyllabic phrase *hōo lâng* (passive marker, lit. 'give man') is commonly realized as a fused syllable [hoŋ] in everyday speech.

(7)   *I*   *hōo*   *lâng*   *phah.*
         3rd sg.   give   man   hit   'He was hit'
         syllable fusion: /i^1 **ho^7 laŋ^5** pʰaʔ^4/→[i^7 **hoŋ^5** pʰaʔ^4]

The intermediate boundary of the TSG is realized through the positioning of base tones. In addition to being an indicator of morphological structure and syntactic phrasing (Chen, 1987), base tones can also act as a highlighting marker through prosodic grouping, as shown in (8). By inserting a TSG boundary after *guá* '1st sg.' and setting it apart from the following verb *mn̄g* 'ask' in the highlighting version, the word reverts to its base tone and receives a narrow focus.

(8)   *Uānn*   *guá*   *mn̄g*   *--ah.*
         change   1st sg.   ask   PART   '(It's) my turn/MY TURN to ask'
         no highlighting: /ũã^7 **gu̯a^2** mŋ̍^{7} aʔ^4/→[ũã^3 **gu̯a^1** mŋ̍^{7} aʔ]$_{TSG}$
         highlighting *guá*:   /ũã^7 **gu̯a^2** mŋ̍^{7} aʔ^4/→[ũã^3 **gu̯a^2**]$_{TSG}$ [mŋ̍^{7} aʔ]$_{TSG}$

adapted from Peng and Beckman (2003)

The highest level of prosodic disjuncture in Taiwanese is the IP boundary, which is considered the largest phonological unit in a language (Jun, 2005). Although its internal structure remains to be explored, previous studies showed some consensus on how such a boundary could be elicited in Taiwanese. Besides absolute utterance-final positions, both vocatives (Pan, 2007c; Pan & Tai, 2006) and subordinate clauses (Hsu & Jun, 1998) have been used in read speech elicitation, as shown in (9) and (10).

(9)   [*A-pah*]$_{IP}$ [*lâi-khì*   *tńg*   *--ah.*]$_{IP}$ (Pan, 2007c)
         Dad   leave   return   PART   'Dad, let's go home!'
         /a^1.paʔ^4 lai̯^{5}.kʰi^3 tŋ^2 aʔ^4/→[a^7.paʔ^4 lai̯^{7}.kʰi^1 tŋ^2 aʔ]

(10)   [*Pîng-iú*   *kóng*]$_{IP}$ [*ta-ke*   *m̄-bián*   *tsiap--lâi.*]$_{IP}$
         friend   say   mother-in-law   not-have-to   bring-home
         '(My) friend said (I) don't have to bring (my) mother-in-law home.'
         /pi̯əŋ^5.i̯u^2 koŋ^2 ta^1.ke^1 m̩^{7}.ben^2 tsi̯ap^4.lai^5/→[pi̯əŋ^7.i̯u^2 koŋ^1 ta^7.ke^1 m̩^{3}.ben^1 tsi̯ap^4.lai̯]

adapted from Hsu and Jun (1998)

Table 15 Break indices in the TW-ToBI
labeling system (Peng & Beckman, 2003).

BI	Description
b4	IP boundary
b3	TSG boundary
b3m	percept of TSG without base tone
b2m	base tone without percept of TSG
b2	syllable boundary
b1	resyllabification
b0m	syllable fusion

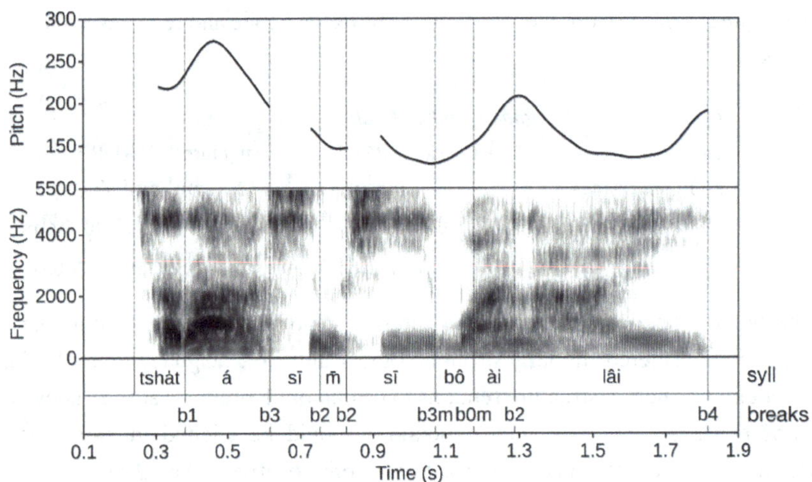

Figure 6 A rendition of *tshàt-á sī m̄ sī bô ài lâi* 'Is it true that the thief does not
want to come?'.

2.5.2 Labeling for Prosodic Grouping

Peng and Beckman (2003) set up a labeling scheme of break indices (BIs) to
label the three levels of prosodic boundaries. In their system, each syllable is
designated a BI, which gauges the disjuncture between the current syllable and
the next. As shown in Table 15, the three levels of boundaries are designated as
b2, b3, and b4 in an ascending order. An example is given in Figure 6. The
whole utterance constitutes one IP. Therefore, the sentence-final syllable *lâi*
'come' is followed by a b4. The phrase *tshàt-á* 'thief' forms a TSG, as the final
syllable diminutive suffix *á* is lengthened and realized with a high-falling base
tone. Therefore, it is followed by a b3. Syllables like the first *sī* 'yes', *m̄* 'no',

and *ài* 'want', which assume their sandhi tones and do not show much lengthening, are thus followed by a b2.

Besides labels for the three prosodic boundaries, there are other BIs in the system to accommodate some of their variants. Break index b0m is used for syllable fusion. The bisyllabic phrase *bô ài* ('do not want, lit. no want') in Figure 6 is realized as a fused syllable so that /bə.ai̯/ becomes [bu̯ai̯]. The syllable *bô* is thus labeled a b0m. Break index b1 is used to label resyllabification. The *tshàt-á* 'thief' in Figure 6 is a good example. The final /t/ in the first syllable *tshàt* 'thief' is geminated and resyllabified as the onset of the second syllable *-á* 'diminutive suffix' so that /tsʰat.a/ becomes [tsʰal.la] instead (Chang, 1989; Chung, 1996). As a result, the break after the syllable *tshàt* is designated a b1.

The three levels of prosodic boundaries are accompanied by gradient phonetic cues. At the right edge of a prosodic phrase, both final lengthening and boundary pause are longer at IP than TSG boundaries, and final lowering is more drastic at boundaries higher in hierarchy (Kuo, 2011, 2012; Pan & Tai, 2006; Peng, 1997). One can also see the effect of prosodic hierarchy on syllable duration from Figure 6. In the utterance, the IP-final syllable *lâi* 'come' is much longer than the TSG-final syllable *-á* 'diminutive suffix', which is in turn longer than the regular syllables of the first *sī* 'yes', *m̄* 'no', and *ài* 'want'. Voice quality also plays a role. Intonational phrase boundaries are often accompanied by a breathy or creaky voice while smaller boundaries are more modal (Kuo, 2012). Segmental information can code prosodic hierarchy as well. Nasals at IP boundaries are often accompanied by inhalation and tend to have a longer nasal plateau and nasal airflow than those at smaller boundaries (Pan, 2007c).

Hierarchical cues are also found at the left edge of a prosodic phrase. Duration again plays a role, but in a trend that is opposite from the right edge. Syllables at IP boundaries tend to be shorter than those at TSG boundaries, and word-initial and -internal syllables are the longest of all (Pan & Tai, 2006). In contrast, the F0 trend patterns in a similar fashion as the right edge (Pan, 2007b; Pan & Tai, 2006). Falling tones tend to have a larger pitch excursion by lowering the pitch floor at higher boundaries, and their falling velocity is also higher. Segments are hierarchically coded as well. Voiceless stops have a longer closure at IP than TSG boundaries, and prenasalization commonly found in voiced stops is accompanied by longer nasal airflow at higher boundaries (Hayashi, Hsu & Keating, 1999; Hsu & Jun, 1998).[5] Interestingly, voice onset time (VOT) measurements across stops show paradigmatic strengthening at larger

---

[5] Hayashi, Hsu, and Keating (1999) did not include the TSG boundary as part of their hierarchical structure due to its violation of the strict layer hypothesis (see later in this section), but instead included a *small phrase* and a *word* boundary, both of which end with a TSG boundary. Since their

disjunctures. Aspirated stops have the longest voice lag at IP boundaries and the shortest at syllable boundaries, while voiced stops have the longest voice lead at IP boundaries and the shortest at syllable boundaries. Not much hierarchical effect is observed for unaspirated stops. In other words, VOTs for voiced, unaspirated, and aspirated stops are coordinated so that they become more distinct from one another at higher boundaries.

Despite the phonetic evidence, not everyone agrees with the organization of the hierarchy. Among the three levels, the TSG boundary is the most controversial (Hsu & Jun, 1996; Pan, 2007b). As mentioned, the application of the tone sandhi rules is to a large extent determined by morphology and syntax, not prosody. In addition, TSG is not strictly layered under IP. Utterance (10) is a good example. Although the first IP ends at *kóng* 'say', the word usually does not coincide with the TSG boundary, as reporting verbs are more commonly realized with a sandhi tone than a base tone. This suggests that TSG violates the strict layer hypothesis assumed in Selkirk's (1986) prosodic organization, and is thus probably not a fully legitimate candidate for the prosodic hierarchy.[6]

Peng and Beckman (2003) also acknowledged the peculiarity of TSGs, and have built this into the break indices of their TW-ToBI labeling system. As shown in Table 15, b2m is used for word-internal syllables that do not undergo tone sandhi rules. This occurs in a few words of a subject-predicate structure, as in *tē-tāng* /te^7.taŋ^7/→[te^7.taŋ^7] 'earthquake, lit. earth-move'. Although the first syllable *tē* is nonfinal, it is realized with a base tone instead of a sandhi tone, and is thus designated b2m. Break index b3m is another example demonstrating the unusual characteristics of TSG boundaries. It is used for intermediate disjunctures that end with a sandhi tone instead of a base tone. Figure 6 shows such an example. There is an intermediate boundary after *sī m̄ sī* 'a grammatical construction for yes-no questions, lit. yes-no-yes', which is evidenced by the lengthening of the second *sī*. However, the syllable is realized with the low-falling sandhi tone instead of the mid-level base tone. It is thus designated a b3m to accommodate the mismatch. As b2m and b3m are proposed alongside the regular indices of b2, b3, and b4 in the TW-ToBI system, it suggests that Peng and Beckman (2003) also recognize the dual morphosyntactic and prosodic functions of TSG boundaries. It also implies that the intermediate disjuncture in Taiwanese is mostly accompanied by a TSG boundary, but can grammatically do without on some occasions.

---

results did not show phonetic gradation between the two levels, the two are grouped together and termed as the TSG boundary here for the sake of simplicity.

[6] The strict layer hypothesis proposed by Selkirk (1986) assumes that prosodic constituents are arranged in a strictly hierarchical manner. In the Taiwanese case, the hypothesis would assume that the IP boundary dominates the TSG boundary under all circumstances.

The results in Pan and colleagues (2018) also support this view. They studied prosodic boundaries of different sizes in spontaneous speech, and found that none of them completely coincide with TSG boundaries. However, there is a positive correlation between prosodic hierarchy and TSG. Larger boundaries tend to be accompanied by TSG boundaries more often than smaller ones, although cross-dialectal differences do exist (IP: 50–80 percent; intermediate: 50–70 percent; word boundaries: 30 percent; syllable boundaries: ≤ 10 percent). In other words, a TSG could be deemed as a prosodic boundary marker due to its gradient nature, much like the more commonly cited phonetic cues, such as initial strengthening, final lengthening, and final lowering.

Based on these studies, it seems safe to assume three levels of prosodic boundaries in Taiwanese. However, the defining features of the intermediate disjuncture are less clear. Peng and Beckman (2003) chose the obvious TSG as the main characteristic of the intermediate level, while at the same time allowing for exceptions to accommodate for the inconsistencies between TSG and Selkirk's (1986) strict layer hypothesis. On the other hand, Hsu and colleagues adopted the "small phrase" (Hayashi et al., 1999) and "word" (Hsu & Jun, 1998) as alternatives for the intermediate disjuncture. Although this indeed bypasses the dilemma faced by Peng and Beckman (2003), it is also problematic in its own right, as they did not provide clear definitions for a small phrase, and the adoption of a word as part of the prosodic hierarchy inevitably requires recourse to TSG. Further studies are thus necessary in order to shed light on the nature of the intermediate disjuncture in Taiwanese.

2.5.3 Prosodic Prominence and Its Labeling

Turning to the other pillar of prosody, one finds prominence in Taiwanese to be mainly realized through tonal realization. Peng and Beckman (2003) mentioned two ways of highlighting in the language. One is through the manipulation of the phonological tone sandhi rules, as illustrated in (8). Certain syllables commonly realized as sandhi tones could be deliberately changed back to their base tones to create a highlighting effect of narrow focus. This is also supported by Pan and colleagues (2018), as they found a negative correlation between the occurrence of base tones and word frequency. Rare words in spontaneous speech, which are also more likely to be highlighted, tend to end in base tones rather than sandhi tones. This implies that the intermediate TSG boundary of Taiwanese could serve a dual role of both prosodic grouping and highlighting, and the former can at times become a way to achieve the latter.

Table 16 Stress labels in the TW-ToBI labeling system
(Peng & Beckman, 2003).

Stress	Description
s2	syllable with fully realized tone
s1	syllable with some tonal reduction
s0	syllable that has lost its tonal specification

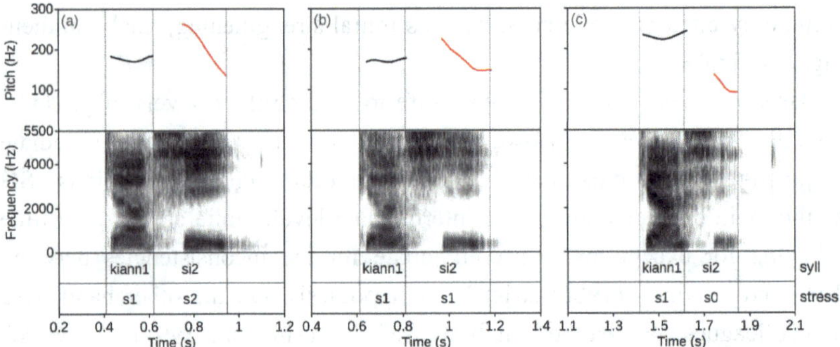

Figure 7 Three renditions of *kiann-sí* 'afraid of dying; coward; scared to death',
with the second syllable *sí* 'to die' being realized as (a) s2, (b) s1, and (c) s0.
Black pitch contours represent the tone realization of *kiann* 'afraid' while red
ones represent the realization of *sí*, for which the base tone is a high-falling tone.

The other highlighting device is through the phonetic realization of tones,
termed stress in Peng and Beckman's (2003) TW-ToBI system. There are three
levels of stress, and each syllable is designated a stress level (Table 16). When
a syllable is realized with a full tone, it is an s2. This is not prevalent in everyday
speech, and only occurs when there is focal prominence. Instead, most syllables
are realized with some degree of tonal reduction, including tonal undershoot
and duration shortening. Syllables of this type are designated as s1. Finally, s0 is
used when a syllable is reduced and has completely lost its tonal specification.
This often occurs in a prosodically weak position, such as the diminutive suffix
-á in word-medial positions, as in *gín-á-lâng* ('child, lit. child-dim.-human'), or
can be morphologically determined (e.g., *kiann-sí* 'afraid of dying, coward' *vs.*
kiann--sí 'scared to death, lit. afraid-die'). Figure 7 shows three different
renditions of *kiann-sí*. Figure 7a is elicited by putting a narrow focus on
the second syllable of *kiann-sí* 'afraid of DYING (not LIVING)'. The syllable
sí is realized with a full-blown high-falling tone and is thus an s2. Figure 7b is
elicited by putting a broad focus on the whole word of *kiann-sí* 'afraid of dying,

coward'. Here *si* is still realized with a high-falling contour, but the high tonal target is somewhat compromised, and the syllable is thus assigned an s1. Finally, Figure 7c is elicited by neutralizing the tone of the second syllable of *kiann--si* 'scared to death'. The syllable is shortened and loses its high tonal target altogether and is thus assigned an s0.

Like boundary cues, duration and pitch both play a role in the phonetic realization of stress (Pan, 2007a). S2 syllables tend to be longer than s1, and this lengthening effect interacts with syllable positioning. Those that are nearer the end of an utterance tend to show a stronger effect. S2 syllables also have a larger F0 range and a higher mean F0 than s1 syllables, and the two cues seem to complement each other. However, in general, duration is still a more reliable cue of stress than pitch.

Unlike many stress-timed Indo-European languages, in which some kind of a highlighting device is obligatory to a prosodic phrase (Jun, 2005), prominence does not play as big of a role in Taiwanese prosody. Although Peng and Beckman's (2003) labeling system requires each syllable to be assigned a stress level, there is no stipulation with regards to the minimal number of any stress level within a phrase. In other words, highlighting is not grammatically essential, and a phrase can be realized without a single s2 syllable. One suspects that this has to do with the nature of tone languages. As pitch has already been largely occupied by the realization of lexical tones, there is little room for pitch manipulation that only serves a structuring purpose. Similar patterns are found in tone languages like Mandarin (Peng et al., 2005) and Cantonese (Wong, Chan & Beckman, 2005). However, this does not mean a prominence-cueing device is lacking altogether in Taiwanese. Rather, both stress (e.g., s2) and boundary signals (e.g., TSG boundaries) contribute when highlighting is necessary for pragmatic purposes.

3 Dialectal Variations in Taiwanese

In addition to the mainstream Taiwanese, there are also several dialectal variations with regard to Taiwanese phonetics. In the following, major variations of consonants, vowels, and tones are introduced.

3.1 Variations in Consonants

Because consonants have specific anchor points for their places of articulation, their pronunciation is relatively stable. The one consonant in Taiwanese that shows substantial dialectal variation is the voiced sibilant /dz/. As mentioned, voiced sibilants are physiologically strenuous to produce (Ohala, 1983).

Therefore, ease of articulation provides a strong motivation for this sound to change.

Across dialects, /dz/ is not always existent, even among old speakers (Ang, 2003, 2012). The Mix variety is the most conservative, and its old speakers still predominantly retain [(d)z] (Table 17). On the other hand, Pro-Tsuan is the most progressive, and its old speakers almost exclusively use [l] instead. The Pro-Tsiang dialect is somewhere in between. Both [(d)z] and [l] are adopted as major free variants among old speakers. For the younger generation, some of the dialectal variations have been blurred (Chuang & Fon, 2017a). The realization of /dz/ in all three dialects is partly dependent on the rounding of the following vowel. In rounded environments, [l] is now the predominant realization, and little variability is observed. Realizations other than [l] became rather marginal. For unrounded environments, more variability is found. The Mix dialect is still the most conservative, and [(d)z] is still a robust realization, along with [l] and [g]. For Pro-Tsiang, [l] and [d] are used interchangeably, but [(d)z] is still used, albeit to a lesser extent. For Pro-Tsuan, [l] is always the dominant form, but [d] can also occasionally occur.

It is interesting that two new realizations, [ʐ] and [d], are found among the younger generation for /dz/. They are not necessarily the dominant realizations, but their appearance is worth mentioning. The retroflex [ʐ] probably arose from negative transfer from the official language Mandarin, which includes a rich set of retroflexes in its consonant inventory. As mentioned, due to the Mandarin-only policy, the younger generation in Taiwan is almost always more dominant in Mandarin than Taiwanese (Chen, 2010a; Yap, 2018). Therefore, it is not surprising for them to adopt [ʐ] as a way to realize /dz/, as both are voiced sibilants by nature. The adoption of [d] is even more intriguing. It is suspected that this has to do with the fact that Taiwanese lacks a /d/ in its voiced stop set, and the use of [d] might be a way for the speakers to fill in the gap for the system.

Table 17 Realizations of /dz/ across dialects and age groups (Ang, 2003, 2012; Chuang & Fon, 2017a). R: rounded; U: unrounded; $A > B$: A is more common than B; $A \gg B$: A is predominant, B is marginal; $A \approx B$: A and B are approximately equal.

	Pro-Tsuan	**Pro-Tsiang**	**Mix (mainstream)**
Old	[l] ≫ [(d)z]	R: [(d)z] ≈ [l] U: [(d)z] ≈ [l] ≫ [g]	R: [(d)z] ≫ [l] U: [(d)z] ≫ [l], [g]
Young	R: [l] ≫ [ʐ] U: [l] > [d]	R: [l] ≫ [ʐ] U: [l] ≈ [d] > [(d)z]	R: [l] ≫ [d] U: [(d)z] ≈ [l] ≈ [g] > [d]

Besides dialectal influences, gender and speaker proficiency are also influential factors (Chuang & Fon, 2018). Males are more inclined to retain the voiced sibilant feature and use [(d)z] and [z] as realizations of /dz/, while females are more inclined to adopt the weakened form [l]. Those with higher proficiency are more likely to retain [g] and [z], while those with lower proficiency are more likely to adopt [l] and [d]. It thus seems safe to say that the future fate of /dz/ is still not yet completely determined. If the two newly adopted forms, [z] and [d], are gaining popularity, or if speakers (especially males) are consciously regaining their language proficiency in response to the reversing language shift movements currently promoted by the government, then the phoneme /dz/ could still survive in one form or another. However, if the weakening process is strong enough to override all other possibilities, then in the near future, Taiwanese will be left with only seventeen consonants (cf. Table 3), and /dz/ will be merged with /l/.

3.2 Variations in Vowels

Compared to consonants, vowels tend to vary much more. In this section, two common vowel variations are examined. One is the oral vowel /ə/ and the other is the nasal vowel /ĩũ̃/. They are chosen because their variations are still fairly widespread among the younger generation and therefore are likely to influence the future path of Taiwanese.

3.2.1 Oral Vowel /ə/

Although /ə/ is currently a phoneme in the vowel system of mainstream Taiwanese (Figure 3 in Section 2.2), it is conjectured to be originally derived from a former phoneme /o/ through delabialization (Chang, 2000; Chen, 2009a; Tung, 1991). In other words, the current /ə/-/ɔ/ contrast was previously an /o/-/ɔ/ contrast instead, resulting in an asymmetric six-vowel system (Figure 8a) (Chen, 2004). The two

Table 18 Realization percentages of the vowel(s) in the mid-central/back region of the vowel space (Hsu, 2016). /o/-/ɔ/: distinction between /o/ and /ə/; /ə/-/ɔ/: distinction between /ə/ and /ɔ/; /ə/-/ɔ/$_M$: distinction between /ə/ and /ɔ/ influenced by Mandarin; /ɔ/: only /ɔ/ in the region.

	Northern	**Central**	**Southern**
Old	/o/-/ɔ/: 100%	/o/-/ɔ/: 55%	/ə/-/ɔ/: 100%
		/ə/-/ɔ/: 45%	
Young	/ə/-/ɔ/$_M$: 55%	/ə/-/ɔ/$_M$: 61%	/ə/-/ɔ/$_M$: 62.5%
	/ɔ/: 40%	/ə/-/ɔ/: 28%	/ə/-/ɔ/: 37.5%

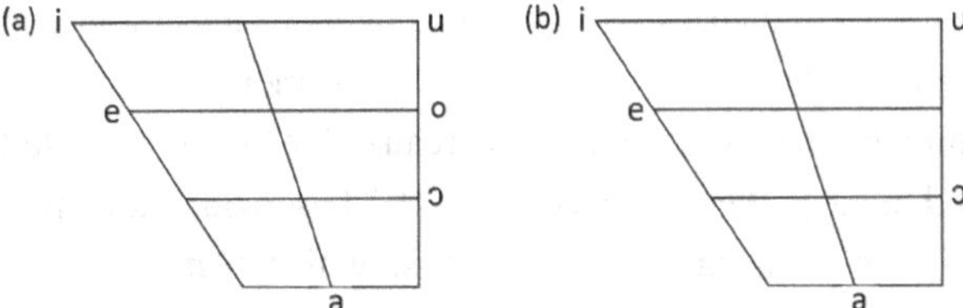

Figure 8 (a) An asymmetric six-vowel system and (b) a symmetric five-vowel system proposed by Chen (2010b).

contrasts are geographically neatly distributed among members of the older generation (Table 18) (Hsu, 2016). Northern speakers use the /o/-/ɔ/ contrast exclusively while southern speakers use only the /ə/-/ɔ/ contrast. On the other hand, central speakers, residing geographically in the middle, occupy the middle ground by showing a mixture of the two, and both /o/-/ɔ/ and /ə/-/ɔ/ contrasts can be observed.

For the younger generation, dialectal variations regarding the mid-central/back vowel contrast is largely attenuated. As shown in Table 18, except for 40 percent of the northern young speakers, who lost their parents' /o/-/ɔ/ contrast by merging the former with the latter, resulting in a symmetric five-vowel system (Figure 8b) (Chen, 2004),[7] the majority of the speakers follow mainstream Taiwanese and show the /ə/-/ɔ/ contrast regardless of geographical location. However, most of these instances are not etymologically justified, but are instead influenced by Mandarin. Table 19 shows some examples of Taiwanese words containing the vowel in concern that also have cognates in Mandarin. These words are commonly produced with an /ɔ/ vowel in the north and /ə/ vowel in the south among old speakers (Hsu, 2016). For the younger generation, however, the choice of /ɔ/ or /ə/ is not determined by geographical location, but is largely determined by the Mandarin pronunciations of the words instead. If the Mandarin cognate has a vowel close to /ɔ/, as is the case of *só* 'lock', then /sɔ/ is preferred over /sə/. On the other hand, if the Mandarin cognate has a vowel close to /ə/, as in *ko* 'older brother', then /kə/ is preferred over /kɔ/ instead.

Based on these examples, it is probably safe to say that the symmetric six-vowel system in mainstream Taiwanese (Figure 3 in Section 2.2), although relatively new, is here to stay, as it has support from the sheer number of speakers due to both geographical locations (for old speakers) and Mandarin influence (for young speakers). The symmetric five-vowel system created by merging /ɔ/ and /o/ might also have a chance of survival (Figure 8b) (Chen, 2004). According

---

[7] Although the vowel chart in Figure 8b is not exactly symmetrical, we are following Chen's (2004) terminology here.

Table 19 Cognates showing Mandarin influences on the /ə/-/ɔ/ variation in Taiwanese adapted from Hsu (2016). Subscript N: the form is etymologically from northern Taiwan; subscript S: the form is etymologically from southern Taiwan.

Word	Gloss	Taiwanese	Mandarin	Preferred
só	'lock'	/sɔ/ₙ, /sə/ₛ	/su̯o/	/sɔ/
kó	'fruit'	/kɔ/ₙ, /kə/ₛ	/ku̯o/	/kɔ/
ko	'older brother'	/kɔ/ₙ, /kə/ₛ	/kɤ/	/kə/
hô	'river'	/hɔ/ₙ, /hə/ₛ	/xɤ/	/hə/
thô	'peach'	/tʰɔ/ₙ, /tʰə/ₛ	/tʰau̯/	no preference
pò	'to report'	/pɔ/ₙ, /pə/ₛ	/pau̯/	no preference

to Chen (2009a, 2009b), both systems are symmetric and are therefore phonologically stable. The old asymmetric six-vowel system would probably gradually disappear, not only because it is phonologically unstable (Chen, 2010b), but also because of the dwindling population of the old generation (Figure 8a) (Hsu, 2016).

3.2.2 Nasal Vowel /ĩũ̯/

The /ĩũ̯/ sound in mainstream Taiwanese is homogeneous across most regions in Taiwan, except for Tainan. Instead of /ĩũ̯/, Tainan speakers use a slightly different vowel /ĩɔ̃/ (Chen, 2009a; Tung, 1991). Table 20 shows some examples.

Although this is a sound that is specific only to the Tainan variety, it is still worth mentioning for two reasons. First, by incorporating /ĩɔ̃/ instead of /ĩũ̯/ in the system, the Tainan variety has created a mismatch between its nasal and oral vowels, violating the universal tendency for nasal vowels to show the same distribution as their oral counterparts (Clements et al., 2015). The universal tendency holds true for mainstream Taiwanese, which includes both /ĩũ̯/ and /iu̯/ in the system (Table 6). However, the Tainan variety poses as an exception, as it allows /iu̯/ but not /ĩũ̯/, and includes /ĩɔ̃/ but not /iɔ̯/. Second, the Tainan variety has been playing a very important role in the development of Taiwanese. Tainan used to be the political center of Taiwan (Liu, 2010), and currently, it is also the only region in Taiwan in which more residents adopt Taiwanese as their primary or secondary language than Mandarin (National Statistics ROC, 2021). Therefore, compared to other parts of Taiwan, Tainan speakers probably have exerted more influence on the development of Taiwanese. However, studies have shown a positive correlation between speaker age and the usage of /ĩɔ̃/ (Chen, 2009a). Younger speakers are more inclined to be mainstreamed to /ĩũ̯/ than to maintain the local /ĩɔ̃/. This suggests that universal tendency and/or the mainstream variety are strong forces in

Table 20 Examples comparing mainstream /ĩũ̃/
and Tainan /ĩɔ̃/.

Word	Gloss	Mainstream	Tainan
siunn	'box'	/sĩũ̃/	/sĩɔ̃/
iûnn	'sheep, goat'	/ĩũ̃/	/ĩɔ̃/
tsiùnn	'sauce'	/tsĩũ̃/	/tsĩɔ̃/

molding a dialectal system, even when there is a robust group of speakers with an alternative pronunciation. More time is needed to see whether the unique nasal vowel /ĩɔ̃/ will continue to exist in the future.

3.3 Variations in Tones

Tones in Taiwanese can also be susceptible to dialectal changes. In this section, two variations regarding tones are introduced. One is the realization of Tone 8, and the other is a tone sandhi rule regarding Tone 5 commonly found in Pro-Tsuan.

3.3.1 Realization of Tone 8

Although Tone 8 is canonically a high short tone (Table 7), its realizations can be highly variable. Table 21 compares several studies that looked at the realizations of Tone 8. It is evident from the table that there is a robust age effect. For the older generation, the realization of Tone 8 is dialect-dependent. Pro-Tsiang seems to be the most consistent. All three locations examined show a mid tone. This implies that Tone 8 is merged into Tone 4 in this dialect. On the other hand, Pro-Tsuan is rather heterogeneous. Depending on the location, realizations can range from a high, to a mid, to a rising tone. The Mix dialect is somewhere in between. All locations show a high tone, but there are also two places that allow a mid tone. This implies that they might be at the early stage of merging.

For the younger generation, however, the dialectal differences are almost completely mitigated. In all except for one instance (Chen, 2009a, 2010b), younger speakers realize Tone 8 as a mid short tone, showing a complete merge between Tone 4 and Tone 8. Notice that this merge only occurs in the base tone. For the sandhi tone, Tone 8 still follows its own sandhi rule. It becomes a Tone 4 when the coda is /p t k/, and becomes a Tone 3 when the coda is /ʔ/.

3.3.2 Tone Sandhi Rule of Tone 5

In mainstream Taiwanese, Tone 5 is realized as a Tone 7 in a sandhi position (Figure 4) (Chang, 1989; Lin, 2001). This is true of both Pro-Tsiang and the Mix dialects. However, for Pro-Tsuan, Tone 5 is realized as a Tone 3 instead

Table 21 Realizations of Tone 8 across the three major dialects.

Major dialect	Location	Old	Young	Studies
Pro-Tsuan	Taipei	high/mid	mid	Chen (2010b, 2013)
Pro-Tsuan	Changhua	high/rising	---	Tu (2011)
Pro-Tsuan	Hsinchu	high/rising	mid	Chen (2018)
Pro-Tsuan	Taichung	mid	mid	Chen (2021)
Pro-Tsiang	Changhua	mid	mid	Chen (2010b)
Pro-Tsiang	Yilan	mid	mid	Chen (2014, 2017)
Pro-Tsiang	Taichung	mid	mid	Chen (2021)
Mix	Hualien	high/mid	---	Chen & Chen (2020)
Mix	Tainan	high/mid	mid/falling	Chen (2009a, 2010b)
Mix	Tainan	high	---	Yang (1988)
Mix	Kaohsiung	high	---	Ang (1997)
Mix	Kaohsiung	high	mid	Khng (2014)

Table 22 Examples of mainstream and Pro-Tsuan Tone 5.

Word	Gloss	Mainstream	Pro-Tsuan	Gloss
sîng-kong	/siŋ^5.kɔŋ^1/	[siŋ^7.kɔŋ^1]	[siŋ^3.kɔŋ^1]	'success'
lâng-kheh	/laŋ^5.kʰeʔ^4/	[laŋ^7.kʰeʔ^4]	[laŋ^3.kʰeʔ^4]	'guest'
nâ-kiû	/nã^5.kiu̯^{5}/	[nã^7.kiu̯^{5}]	[nã^3.kiu̯^{5}]	'basketball'

(Lu, 2003; Tung, 1991). Table 22 shows some examples. This rule seems fairly ubiquitous within the dialect, and no difference across age groups was observed (Chen, 2021). It is therefore considered a robust rule and should remain one of the signature characteristics of the dialect for some time to come.

4 Materials for Research on Taiwanese

We would like to make two sets of materials available to researchers interested in the phonetics of Taiwanese. The first is a read speech dataset of *The Story of Aju*, which is a short passage originally designed for studying the phonetic realization of the voiced sibilant /dz/ in Taiwanese (Chuang & Fon, 2017b, 2018). The second is a spontaneous speech dataset of monologues elicited through an interview format. It is part of a large corpus construction project on the spontaneous speech of Mandarin-Taiwanese bilinguals (Fon, 2004).

4.1 *The Story of Aju*

Although read speech elicitation is a common way of obtaining speech data, it is technically more difficult in Taiwanese to do so compared to many other more well-known languages. As the current romanization system (Ministry of Education ROC, 2008) and the standardization of character writing (Ministry of Education ROC, 2014) were only recently introduced, many adult speakers are still not very proficient in the spelling and writing rules and tend to revert to a character-based make-do system when the need for writing Taiwanese arises. This grassroot system is not standardized, can vary from person to person, and is often produced extemporaneously. Therefore, longer passages of read speech are rather difficult to elicit in Taiwanese without substantial experimenter intervention. *The Story of Aju* was created against this backdrop. It is a deliberately short passage of only ninety syllables. However, it includes all oral monophthongs and diphthongs except for /u̯e/ in Taiwanese. Two of the nasal vowels, /ĩ/ and /ĩũ̯/, and both syllabic nasals, /m̩/ and /ŋ̍/, are also included. All onset consonants except for /pʰ/ are included. Finally, all codas are included. The full text of the passage is shown in (11). For the convenience of the readers, both the standard character system and the romanization system are provided, along with a fairly literal English translation. Researchers are encouraged to use whatever writing system they see fit to their own situations.

(11)　　　　有一个因仔叫做阿如。伊足溫柔，毋過字寫甲足穤，所以伊的同學攏共伊笑。頂禮拜二，天氣足熱，阿如想欲入去教室，毋過伊同學共伊欺負，無愛予阿如入去。阿如心內足艱苦，所以轉去共媽媽講。媽媽就共伊講：「阿如，你著愛忍耐！」

Ū tsi̍t ê gín-á kiò-tsò A-jû. I tsiok un-jiû, m̄-koh jī siá kah tsiok bái, sóo-í i ê tông-o̍h lóng kā i tshiò. Tíng lé-pài-jī, thinn-khì tsiok jua̍h, A-jû siūnn-beh ji̍p-khì kàu-sik, m̄-koh i tông-o̍h kā i khi-hū, bô ài hōo A-jû--ji̍p-khì. A-jû sim-lāi tsiok kan-khóo, sóo-í tńg-khì kā ma-ma kóng. Ma-ma tō kā i kóng, "A-jû, lí tio̍h ài jím-nāi!"

There was a child named Aju. She was very sweet, but had poor handwriting, so her classmates all laughed at her. Last Tuesday, it was very hot, and Aju wanted to enter the classroom, but her classmates bullied her by not letting her in. Aju was in anguish, so she went home and told her mom. Mom then told her, "Aju, you just have to put up with it!"

Recordings and textgrid files of Praat of two males and two females are made available for public use (M1.wav, M1.TextGrid, M2.wav, M2.TextGrid, F1.wav, F1.TextGrid, F2.wav, F2.TextGrid). All speakers were young Mandarin-Taiwanese early bilinguals who have acquired Min since birth. To gauge their Min proficiency, two sets of self-ratings on a Likert scale of 1 to 7 were used,

Table 23 Biographical details of the speakers of *The Story of Aju* (Chuang & Fon, 2017b, 2018). AoA: age of acquisition of Min; proficiency (Min: Mandarin): 1 = little proficiency, 7 = full proficiency; usage (Min:Mandarin): 1 = rare usage, 7 = frequent usage.

Speaker	Age	Gender	Hometown	AoA	Proficiency	Usage
M1	21	male	Taipei	birth	6:7	4:7
M2	22	male	Changhua	birth	6:7	6:7
F1	23	female	Tainan	birth	6:7	6:7
F2	21	female	Taichung	birth	6:7	6:7

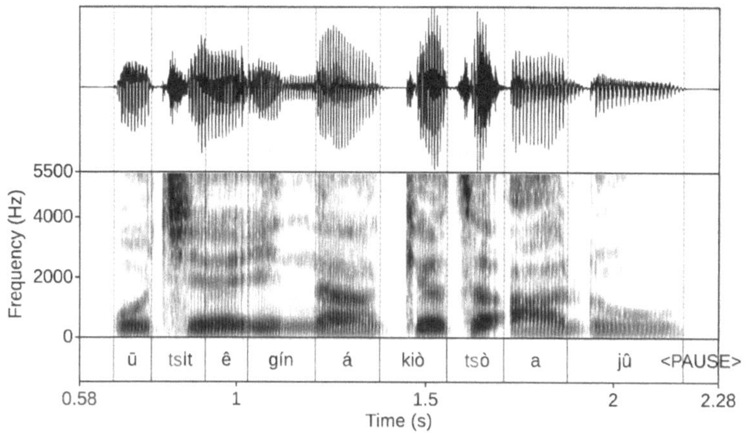

Figure 9 An illustration of Praat labeling for *The Story of Aju* by Subject M2.

one for Mandarin and Min proficiency, and the other for their frequency of use. Ratings for Mandarin were included as a reference since it is the official language in Taiwan, and all speakers of the younger generation are expected to develop full proficiency in the language and use it on a daily basis. Table 23 shows the biographical details of the speakers.

Recordings were done in a sound-treated room using a KORG MR-1000 digital recorder and a Sennheiser HMD 25-1 head-mounted microphone at a sampling rate of 44,100 Hz, and were later downsampled to 22,050 Hz using Adobe Audition CS6. The experimenter was a Mandarin-Taiwanese bilingual native speaker. Before the recording, she checked with each subject to make sure they could produce the paragraph fluently and correctly. Subjects were asked to read in a natural fashion. The recording session lasted less than fifteen minutes.

Figure 9 is an illustration of the labeling of *The Story of Aju* in Praat. Syllables were labeled based on their underlying forms. For example, even though *tsit ê* 'one-CL' is resyllabified as [tɕil.le] in the actual rendition, the labeling still follows the syllable boundaries stipulated by phonology, which is /tɕit.e/.

4.2 The Spontaneous Speech Corpus

The Spontaneous Speech Corpus was constructed to facilitate research on the spontaneous speech of Mandarin-Taiwanese bilinguals in Taiwan, who constitute the largest ethnic group in the country (Huang, 1993). Speech was elicited in an interview format by a fluent Mandarin-Taiwanese bilingual experimenter in a quiet room using SONY TCD-D8 and a Sennheiser HMD 25-1 head-mounted microphone at a sampling rate of 44,100 Hz, and was later down-sampled to 22,050 Hz using Adobe Audition CS6. Each speaker contributed roughly thirty minutes of Mandarin and thirty minutes of Taiwanese speech data.

An experimenter usually started off with some neutral preset questions, but was given the liberty to sidetrack into topics that seemed of interest to the speakers along the way. Common topics discussed include hometown, food, travel, movies, and careers. Short excerpts of the Taiwanese recordings and their corresponding Praat TextGrid files from two males and two females are made available for public use (M3.wav, M3.TextGrid, M4.wav, M4.TextGrid, F3. wav, F3.TextGrid, F4.wav, F4.TextGrid). To control for dialectal variations, all speakers were young adults from Taichung, a central metropolitan area in Taiwan. However, it is difficult to pinpoint exactly which dialect they spoke based on their hometowns due to various degrees of dialect mixing shown in the data. Table 24 shows the biographical details of the speakers. In the excerpts, they were all talking about their hometowns. A full transcription of the excerpts is provided in the Appendix.

5 Acoustic Analysis of the Pronunciation of Taiwanese

In this section, we would like to utilize the two sets of data in Section 4 and examine some of the phonetic realizations of the Taiwanese phonological system. We first examined the allophonic variations of onset plosives, the

Table 24 Biographical details of the speakers of the Mandarin-Taiwanese Spontaneous Speech Corpus (Fon, 2004).

Speaker	Age	Gender	Hometown	Recording (mm:ss)
M3	33	male	Qingshui, Taichung	03:16
M4	late 20s	male	Longjing, Taichung	03:04
F3	mid 20s	female	Dongshi, Taichung	03:09
F4	24	female	Taiping, Taichung	03:01

voiced sibilant /dz/, vowels, and coda plosives. Then we looked at realizations of tones and syllable fusion. Finally, we showed how the prosodic structure could be manifested through tone. Please note that the phenomena mentioned were intended to provide a glimpse of how some major elements of Taiwanese phonology are phonetically realized, and were not meant to comprise an exhaustive list. Although some of the number counts in the tables that follow are not large due to the small size of the data provided in Section 4, the phenomena themselves are not fortuitous, but are in fact rather common in at least some dialects of Taiwanese, as per our observations. Many of the characteristics discussed can be developed into one or several full-blown lines of research, and the purpose of this section is to provide some potential pointers for interested researchers to delve deeper into Taiwanese phonetics.

5.1 Onset Plosives

As discussed in Section 2, Taiwanese has nine plosives in total (Table 3) (Chang, 1989). All except for /ʔ/ can act as syllable onsets. In the following, the phonetic realizations of voiced, voiceless unaspirated, and voiceless aspirated plosives are examined in turn.

Table 25 shows the top realizations of voiced /b/ and /g/. In both cases, there are stark differences between read and spontaneous speech. For /b/, the most

Table 25 Distribution of the top allophonic realizations of /b/ and /g/ in read and spontaneous speech. Tokens less than 10 percent are listed under miscellaneous (misc), and subscript numbers indicate their frequency of appearance. Single tokens are not listed. Two methods of calculation were adopted for /g/ in spontaneous speech. The middle section refers to all tokens, while the lower section excludes tokens of the first personal pronouns *guá* '1st pers. sg.' and *guán* '1st pers. pl.' (see text).

	/b/	**/g/**
Read	[b]: 54% [ᵐb]: 23% ($n = 13$)	[ᵑg]: 75% ($n = 8$)
Spontaneous	[b]: 31% [v]: 24% [β]: 22% misc: [m$_4$ ᵐb$_4$ ᵑb$_2$] ($n = 55$)	$\varnothing$: 81% misc: [ᵑg$_9$ g$_3$ ɥ$_3$ ŋ$_2$] ($n = 106$)
Spontaneous (pron. excluded)	---	$\varnothing$: 50% [ᵑg]: 29% misc: [ɥ$_3$ g$_2$] ($n = 28$)

common realization in read speech was the default [b], accounting for 54 percent of the data. The prenasalized [^{m}b] was the second most common, accounting for 23 percent. In contrast, the role of [b] was drastically diminished in spontaneous speech, accounting for only 31 percent of the data, while voiced fricatives [v] and [β] became more common candidates, and accounted for 24 percent and 22 percent, respectively.

Turning to /g/, we found a different picture. First of all, the default [g] was not a common realization for /g/ (Table 25). We found no instance of [g] in read speech, and only three instances in spontaneous speech. Instead, the dominant realization for /g/ in read speech was the prenasalized [^{ŋ}g], accounting for 75 percent of the data, and total deletion was actually the most prevalent "realization" in spontaneous speech, with a deletion rate as high as 81 percent. The prenasalized [^{ŋ}g] came in a far second, accounting for only 8 percent of the data. Careful inspection showed that the predominance of total deletion was largely contributed by the two first personal pronouns, *guá* '1st pers. sg.' and *guán* '1st pers. pl.', which accounted for about 84 percent of the cases. However, deletion was not limited to such, as content words like *Tâi-gí* 'Taiwanese' and *gín-á* 'child' were also found to omit their /g/. Even if personal pronouns were disregarded, deletion is still the most preferred option, accounting for 50 percent of the data, and the prenasalized [^{ŋ}g] is still the second, accounting for 29 percent.

The variability of /b/ and /g/ is higher than what was found in previous studies on careful speech (cf. Pan, 1995), in which only [^{m}b] and [^{ŋ}g] were mentioned, not [v], [β], and total deletion. However, since speakers were encouraged to speak naturally in this study, larger variability was expected. Maintaining voicing throughout closure is a physically strenuous task (Ohala, 1983). Therefore, voiced stops are often either (partially) devoiced to maintain stop closure or become prenasalized or spirantized to maintain voicing.

Based on our data, Taiwanese did not take the route of devoicing, as we found no instance of /b/→[p] and only one instance of /g/→[k]. With three-way voicing contrast in stops, devoicing might potentially jeopardize the between-category discriminability in the language and is thus dispreferred. Instead, when a voiced stop is intended, speakers tend to aim for either the voiced stop itself, its prenasalized variant, or its spirantized version. The latter two are useful for sustaining voicing since they allow an opening in the supralaryngeal cavity, keeping the intraoral pressure low. The adoption of these two alternative pronunciations also implies that voicing is probably a more valued feature than closure for the realization of voiced stops in Taiwanese. Figure 10 shows some spectrographic examples of /b/ realizations.

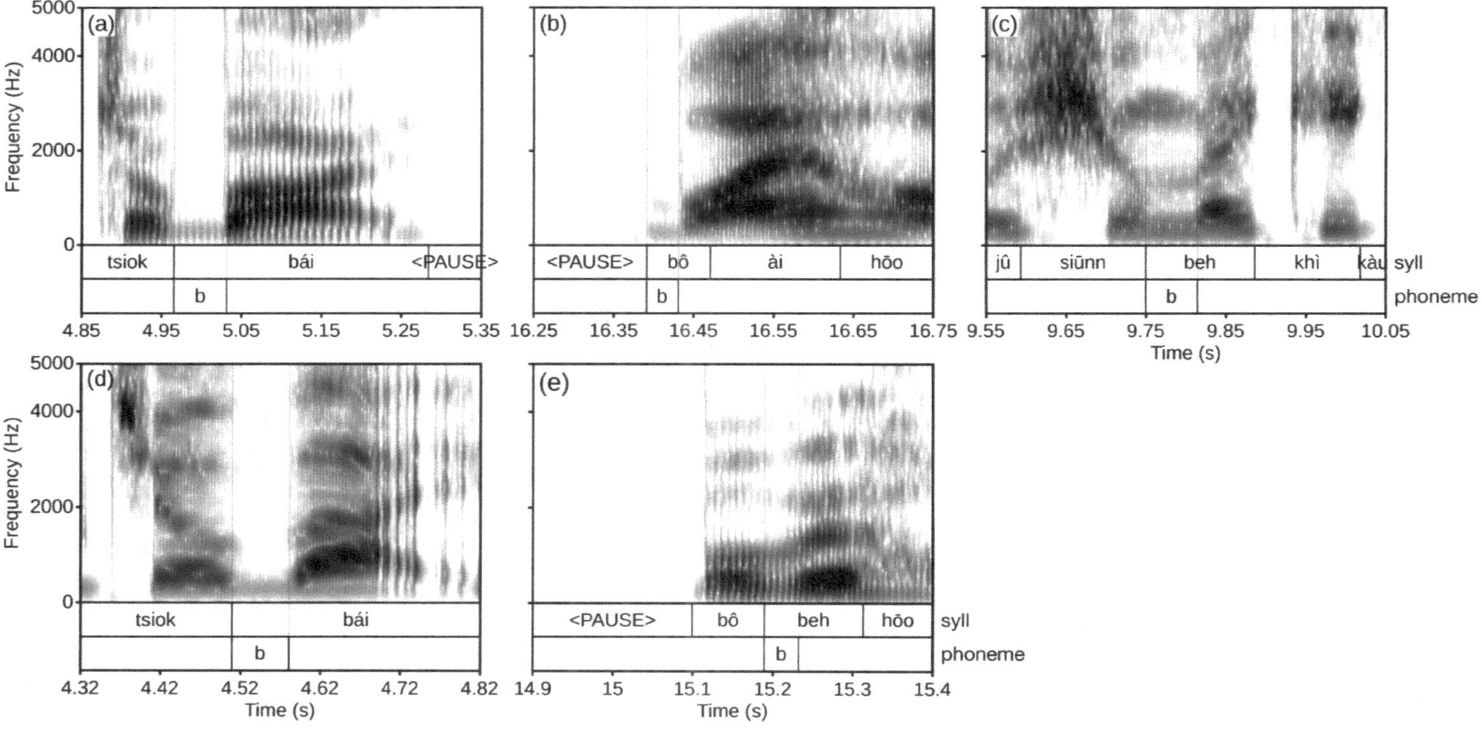

Figure 10 Illustrations of /b/ realized as (a) the original [b] in *tsiok **b**ái* 'very ugly'; (b) a prenasalized [ᵐb] in ***b**ô ài* 'do not want'; (c) a nasal [m] in *siūnn **b**eh* 'want'; (d) a spirantized [v] in *tsiok **b**ái* 'very ugly', and (e) a spirantized [β] in *bô **b**eh* 'do not want'.

The realization difference between /b/ and /g/ was also interesting. In read speech, the default [b] was the most common realization for /b/, while the prenasalized [$^{\eta}$g] was the most common for /g/. In spontaneous speech, the most common realization for /b/ was the spirantized [β, v], while the most common for /g/ was total deletion. In both cases, the realizations of /g/ are more lenited than those of /b/, more so in spontaneous speech than read speech. This shows that the closure of the voiced set is probably gradually eroding away, and the velar position is taking the lead. This is likely due to both physiological and lexical factors. Physiologically, active voicing is harder to maintain in /g/ than in /b/ because of a smaller supralaryngeal cavity and a more limited soft surface on which air pressure can impinge (Ohala, 1983). Lexically, /g/ is also much less productive than /b/ in the language. *TJ's Dictionary of Non-literary Taiwanese* (Tiu^{n}, 2009) included 1,009 entries for /b/-initial words, but only 465 entries for /g/. Similarly, we found twenty-one unique /b/-words in our spontaneous speech corpus, but only eleven /g/-words. Furthermore, if we disregard the two overly represented personal pronouns of *guá* '1st pers. sg.' and *guán* '1st pers. pl.', then there were only twenty-seven tokens containing /g/, as compared to fifty-five tokens containing /b/. All these showed that in terms of both type and token frequencies, /g/ is consistently the lesser used of the two. Therefore, the loss of /g/ might not create as much confusion as losing /b/.

Turning to the voiceless unaspirated set, we seemed to find much less variability (Table 26). For read speech, the default realization was close to 100 percent for all three stops. Even for spontaneous speech, the realization rates were still 70 percent. /t/ and /k/ also had an additional prenasalized voiced allophone of around 10 percent in spontaneous speech. A close inspection

Table 26 Distribution of common allophonic realizations of /p/, /t/, and /k/ in read and spontaneous speech. Tokens less than 10 percent are listed under miscellaneous (misc), and subscript numbers indicate their frequency of appearances. Single tokens are not listed.

	/p/	/t/	/k/
Read	[p]: 100% ($n = 6$)	[t]: 100% ($n = 23$)	[k]: 94% misc: [g_2] ($n = 48$)
Spontaneous	[p]: 70% $\varnothing$: 10% misc: [v_4 b_3] ($n = 50$)	[t]: 73% misc: [$^{n}d_{21}$ d_{12} $\varnothing_{11}$ $ð_7$ h_2 $ɹ_2$] ($n = 232$)	[k]: 82% [$^{\eta}$g]: 10% misc: [$ŋ_6$ g_4] ($n = 184$)

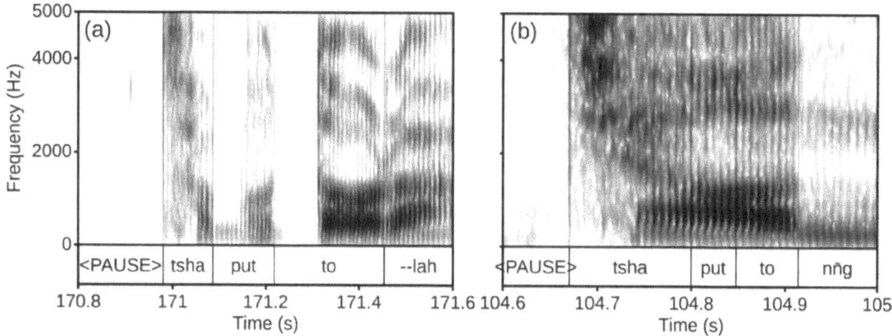

Figure 11 An illustration of the word *tsha-put-to* 'almost' realized in (a) its original trisyllabic form and (b) its coalesced monosyllabic form *tshiâu*.

Table 27 Distribution of common allophonic realizations of /pʰ/, /tʰ/, and /kʰ/ in read and spontaneous speech. Tokens less than 10 percent are listed under miscellaneous (misc), and subscript numbers indicate their frequency of appearances. Single tokens are not listed.

	/pʰ/	/tʰ/	/kʰ/
Read	---	[tʰ]: 100% ($n = 4$)	[kʰ]: 92% ($n = 25$)
Spontaneous	[pʰ]: 100% ($n = 1$)	[tʰ]: 100% ($n = 12$)	[kʰ]: 81% misc: [h$_4$ $\emptyset_3$ ɦ$_2$] ($n = 85$)

showed that more than 90 percent of these cases were due to carryover assimilation from preceding nasals or vowels (e.g., /t/→[ⁿd] in *guán tau* 'my place'). For /p/, there was a secondary realization of total deletion in spontaneous speech. All of them came from a single lexical item, *tsha-put-to* 'about'. Of the seven instances found, five showed some kind of syllable contraction. The trisyllabic word was conventionally coalesced into a monosyllabic *tshiâu* (Figure 11). This shows that total deletion is unlikely to be a regular allophonic realization of /p/, but is rather a result of lexicalized syllable contraction specific to *tsha-put-to*.

Realizations for the aspirated set were even more stable (Table 27). Both /tʰ/ and /kʰ/ were predominantly realized as their respective default [tʰ] and [kʰ] in read and spontaneous speech. Unfortunately, we only collected one case of /pʰ/ in spontaneous speech, and none in read speech, so it is unclear whether /pʰ/ would also have a consistent realization as [pʰ]. However, since labials did not show more variability than the other two places in the voiced (Table 25) and the

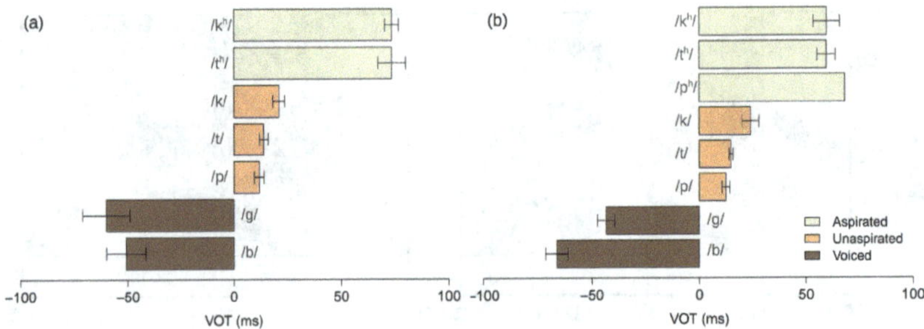

Figure 12 VOT values of onset plosives in (a) read and (b) spontaneous speech. Error bars represent standard errors. No token of /pʰ/ was found in read speech and only one token was found in spontaneous speech. Therefore, no error bar was calculated for /pʰ/.

unaspirated set (Table 26), we would predict that /pʰ/ would also generally be realized as [pʰ].

Figure 12 shows the VOT values of the three sets of onset plosives that were realized as their default in read and spontaneous speech. For voiced stops, since prenasalized realizations were prevalent (Table 25), sometimes even more prevalent than the default realizations, both the default and the prenasalized realizations were included in the VOT calculation. As shown in the figure, the three sets of voiced, voiceless unaspirated, and voiceless aspirated onset stops showed distinct VOT ranges in both read and spontaneous speech. Voiced VOT had an average of −45 ms to −65 ms, voiceless unaspirated VOT had an average of 10 ms to 25 ms, and voiceless aspirated VOT had an average of 60 ms to 75 ms. The results for the voiceless unaspirated set coincided well with most previous studies (Chiung, 2002; Hsieh, 2007; Lin, 2013; Tseng & Huang, 1992), although it was somewhat shorter than those in Huang (2009). For the voiced set, our voice lead was consistent with what was found in Hsieh (2007) and Tseng and Huang (1992), but was longer than that in Huang (2009), and shorter than that in Chiung (2002). Finally, for the voiceless aspirated set, the voice lag in this study was approximately the same as that in Hsieh (2007), but was shorter than that in Chiung (2002), Lin (2013), and Huang (2009), and longer than that in Tseng and Huang (1992). Since all of these studies employed various methodologies, this suggests that the voiceless unaspirated set is the most stable in terms of its VOT measures, probably because it is the set in between the two extremes. Both the voiced and the voiceless aspirated sets are more susceptible to various factors, such as genre, speech rate, and speaker idiosyncrasies. However, it is also clear from previous studies and from Figure 12 that the three-way distinction was largely maintained despite the effect of these performance factors.

5.2 Voiced Sibilant /dz/

The realization of the voiced sibilant /dz/ has been known to be varied (Chuang & Fon, 2017a, 2018). This is not surprising, as it is physiologically a difficult sound to produce (Ohala, 1983). Table 28 shows the common allophonic realizations of /dz/ in read and spontaneous speech. We found four major realizations, [z d l ŋg]. [z] was only observed in read speech. This is expected. Although it is considered one of the canonical pronunciations of /dz/ (Ang, 1997, 2003; Chen, 1995; Lin, 1995), it is also physiologically strenuous (Ohala, 1983), and probably harder to maintain in spontaneous speech. [ŋg] is a dialectal variant, and it only occurs before an unrounded vowel (Ang, 2003). In our corpus, only Subjects F1 and F4 sometimes adopted this variant. [l] is a lenited form of /dz/. It was observed in all four environments, but was more common before rounded than unrounded vowels. In unrounded environments in read speech, only one token was found. [d] also appeared in all environments except before rounded vowels in spontaneous speech. It seems this newly adopted variant is very popular among the younger generation (Chuang & Fon, 2017a, 2018).

There are at least two interesting points from Table 28. First, between the two major traits of the voiced sibilant /dz/, voicing seems to be valued more than frication. Of the 67 /dz/ tokens collected in our corpus, voiced allophonic realizations accounted for more than 90 percent, including all four of the major realizations [z d l ŋg]. On the other hand, there were only thirteen

Table 28 Distribution of the common allophonic realizations of /dz/ before rounded and unrounded vowels in read and spontaneous speech. Tokens with less than 10 percent are listed under miscellaneous (misc), and subscript numbers indicate their frequency of appearances. Single tokens are not listed.

	Rounded	**Unrounded**
Read	[l]: 29% [d]: 25% [z]: 17% misc: [ˈd$_2$ l$_2$] ($n = 24$)	[d]: 36% [ŋg]: 18% [z]: 18% misc: [dz$_2$] ($n = 22$)
Spontaneous	[l]: 100% ($n = 2$)	[d]: 21% [l]: 16% [ŋg]: 16% misc: [ˈd$_2$ ⁿd$_2$] ($n = 19$)

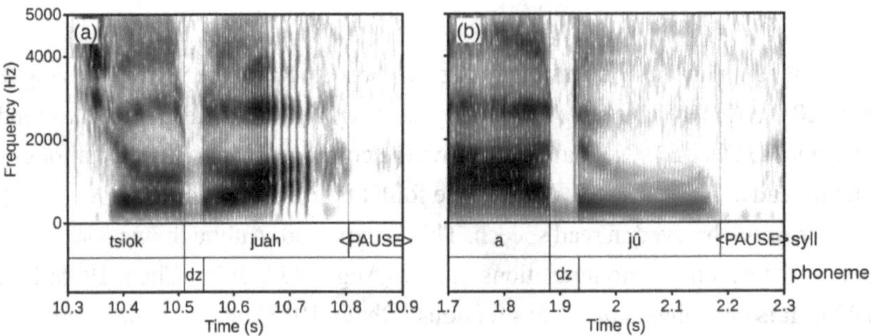

Figure 13 Examples of /dz/ being realized as (a) [l] in *tsiok juàh* 'very hot', and (b) [d] in *A-jû* '(girl's name)'.

tokens of sibilants, including eight [z]'s, two [dz]'s, two [ts]'s, and one [s], accounting for less than 20 percent.[8] In other words, like voiced stops (Table 25), Taiwanese speakers viewed the voicing sound quality as more important to the realization of /dz/ than maintaining the designated manner of articulation. It is possible that voicing itself creates a perceptual similarity between sounds of different manners, which is not easily achieved by sounds of the same manner with different voicing status (Balise & Diehl, 1994). Second, besides the rounded vowels in spontaneous speech, which only had two tokens, [d] was a prominent realization in the remaining three environments. This is especially intriguing, as the modern Taiwanese consonant inventory does not include /d/. However, since [l] is a dominant lenition form for /dz/ (Ang, 2003; Wang, 2014), young speakers nowadays seem to have filled the gap created by the missing /d/ through the realization of /dz/→[l]→[d], thus making the voiced stop series complete (Chuang & Fon, 2017a, 2018). If we consider [d] to be also a realization subtype of [l], then [l] has indeed become the dominant realization of the voiced sibilant /dz/ in Taiwanese, as 61 percent of the tokens were realized either as [l l] or [d ˡd ⁿd] [cf. Ang (2003)]. Acoustically, the two realizations are not that much different either (Figure 13). [d] only has a low-frequency voice bar, while [l] has additional higher-frequency formants. The transition is also slightly more abrupt in [d] than in [l] due to the release of the stop closure. However, the two could potentially be very similar to a native listener's ear.

---

[8] The [s] and one [ts] occurred before a rounded vowel /u/ in *A-jû* '(girl's name)', and the other [ts] occurred before an unrounded vowel /i/ in *--jïp-khì* 'enter'. Since all three only occurred once in their respective tonal environments, they were not listed in Table 28.

5.3 Vowels

As most of our speakers are from central and southern Taiwan, their vowel choices expectedly lean toward the south, with some tokens of the north from time to time. This mixture of both varieties is consistent with the findings in Hsu (2016). Figure 14 shows the normalized values of F1 and F2 of the vowels adopted by the speakers. The vowels were taken from CV and V syllables with a nonnasal onset and an oral vowel. This was to avoid complications in formant smearing caused by nasal formants and anti-formants. Also, since juxtaposition of adjacent vowel targets in diphthongs often results in target undershoot, only monophthongs were included in the calculation. Formant values were first extracted from the midpoint of a vowel by a Praat script, and Lobanov's (1971) normalization was applied using the vowels package (Kendall & Thomas, 2018) in R (R Core Team, 2021).

For read speech, all four speakers adopted the symmetric six-vowel system of /i, e, a, ə, ɔ, u/ (cf. Figure 3), as all etymologically /ə/-tokens except for one were realized as such. The exception was an [ɔ] uttered by M1 in one of the two tokens of *tông-òh* /tɔŋ.əʔ/ 'classmates'. This shows that /ə/ is the dominant vowel in the vowel system for read speech for these speakers. As shown in Figure 14a, the three corner vowels /i, a, u/ demonstrated very little variation. This is probably due to the fact that they are located at the edges of the vowel space, so little variability is allowed. Interestingly, the non-corner vowel /ɔ/ also showed little variation. We suspect that this is because its neighboring vowel /ə/ is too close by, leaving it little room for variability. In contrast, the two mid

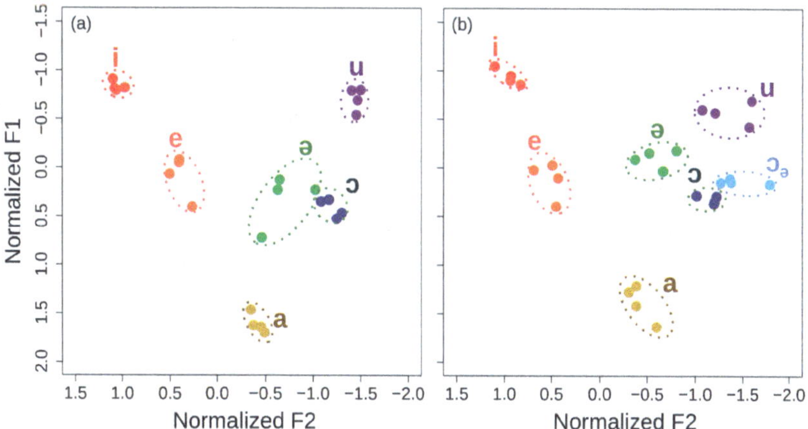

Figure 14 Normalized F1 and F2 values of the vowels adopted by speakers in (a) read and (b) spontaneous speech. Each dot represents the averaged values for that vowel for one speaker. 'ɔ_ə' indicates that the vowel was phonemically an /ə/ but pronounced as [ɔ].

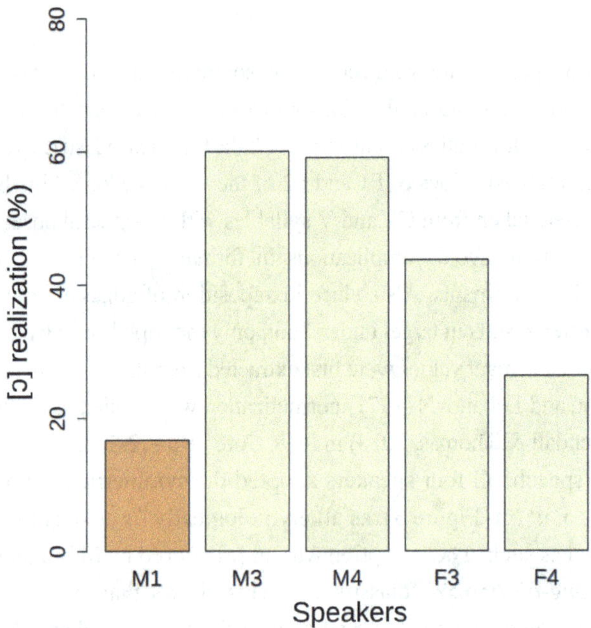

Figure 15 Realization rates of /ə/→[ɔ] among the speakers who had this
allophone. The darker bar is read speech, while the lighter bars
are spontaneous speech.

vowels of /e/ and /ə/ showed larger inter-speaker variation. This is possibly due
to the fact that phonemically there is only one level of mid vowels in Taiwanese
and substantial leeway is allowed.

For spontaneous speech, the picture was somewhat different, and there was
an additional vowel of [ɔ], labeled as [ɔə] (Figure 14b). This was because all
four speakers showed free variation between [ə] and [ɔ] for what should have
been /ə/. Figure 15 displays the [ɔ] realization rates for these speakers. It is
interesting to see a potential gender effect. Both M3 and M4 had a realization
rate of around 60 percent, while F3 had 44 percent and F4 only had 26 percent.

Except for /ə/, all the other vowels in spontaneous speech demonstrated more
variability than their read speech counterparts. This is expected, since coarticu-
lation and reduction are more prevalent due to faster speech rate and higher
spontaneity. /ə/ showed little variation, probably also because it had little room
for variability due to crowdedness in the region.

The fact that different vowel realizations were observed across the two genres
is rather interesting. The predominance of /ə/→[ə] in read speech suggests that
[ə] is probably considered the canonical and dominant form for these speakers.
This is consistent with the claim by Chang (2000) and Tung (2001). On the other

hand, the mixture of [ə] and [ɔ] in spontaneous speech implies that [ɔ] has become an allophone of /ə/, and [ə] and [ɔ] are in free variation. This is in line with Hsu's (2016) findings. Currently, [ə] seems to be winning, as it was the canonical and dominant form in read speech. The fact that females also preferred [ə] over [ɔ] in both genres implies that [ə] does not have a negative connotation, as female speakers usually tend toward more prestigious speech (Labov, 2001). Even though northern speakers generally use /ɔ/ not /ə/ (Hsu, 2016), they also use Taiwanese less often than their central and southern counterparts (National Statistics ROC, 2021), and are thus less likely to exert much influence on the future direction of the language. Therefore, [ə] might still be the dominant and canonical realization of /ə/ for some time to come.

5.4 Coda Obstruents

Taiwanese allows four obstruents /p t k ʔ/ in the coda position (Chang, 1989). Previous studies suggested a tendency for the final obstruents to be deleted, and omission is both segment- and tone-dependent. It tends to be more common for the glottal /ʔ/ than for the oral /p t k/, and more common for Tone 8 than Tone 4 for /ʔ/ (Chen, 2009b, 2010b; Pan & Lyu, 2021).

Figure 16 shows the realization of the obstruent codas in our data. "Regular" refers to realizations dictated by phonological rules. This includes the default [p t k ʔ] realizations, the intervocalic lenition of [p], [t], and [k] into [β], [l] and [ɣ], respectively, the word-medial deletion of [ʔ], and the realizations of anticipatory assimilation to the following sound. Figure 17 shows some examples for the realizations of /k/. Figure 17a is a default instance of [k] in *sann ê a-tsik* 'three uncles, lit. three CL uncle', Figure 17b is a lenition example of /k/ →[ɣ] in

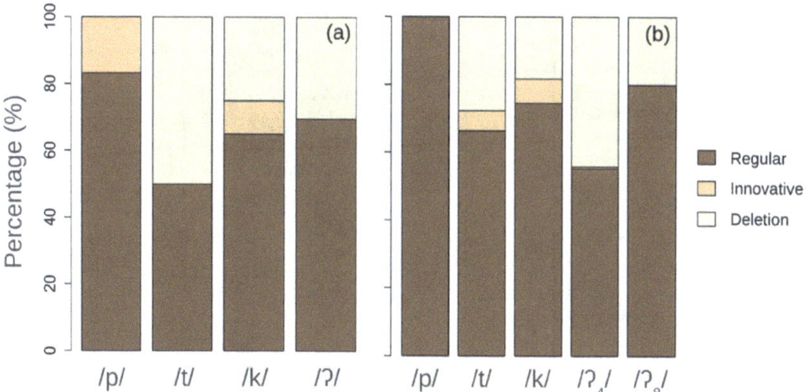

Figure 16 Percentage realizations of coda obstruents /p t k ʔ/ in (a) read and (b) spontaneous speech. Subscript numbers after /ʔ/ in (b) indicate tone numbers.

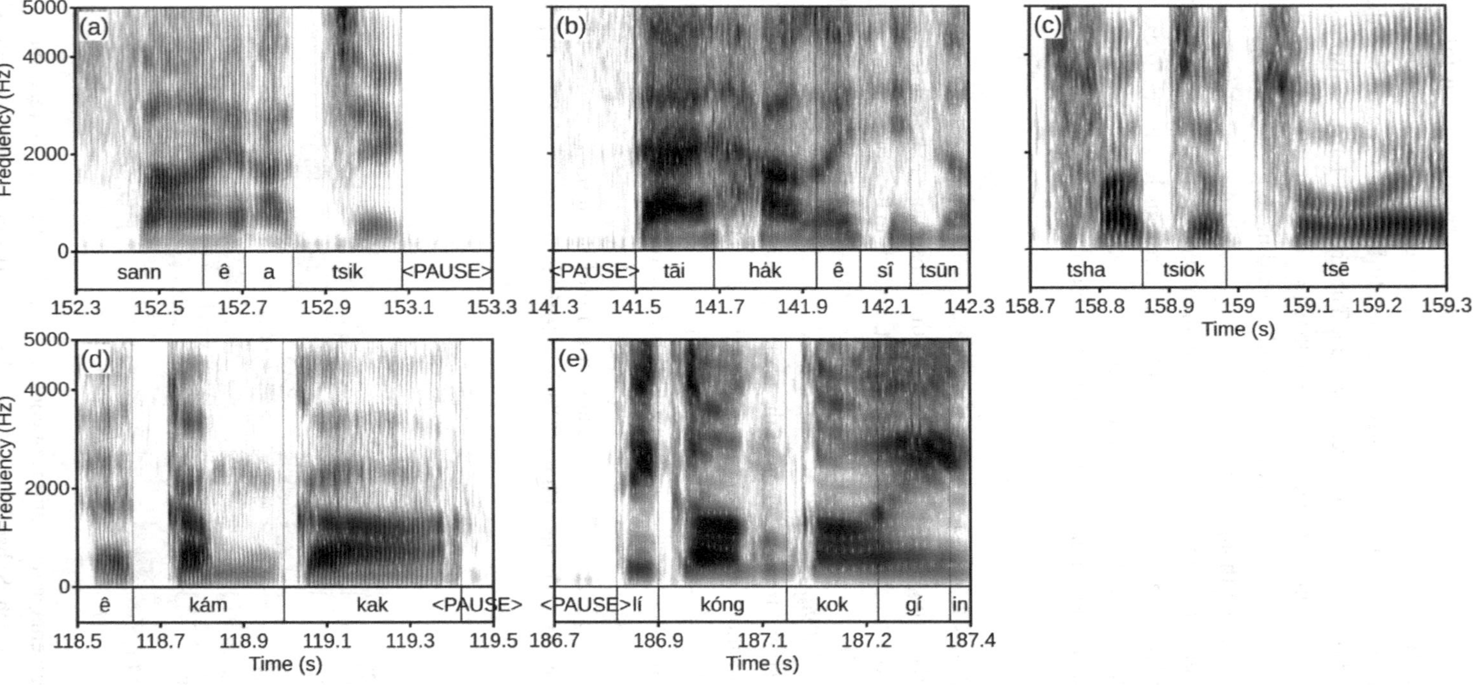

Figure 17 An example of different realizations of the final /k/: (a) default realization of /k/→[k] in *sann ê a-tsik* 'three uncles, lit. three CL uncle'; (b) lenition of /k/→[ɣ] in *tāi-hȧk ê sî-tsūn* 'during college, lit. college GEN time'; (c) anticipatory assimilation of /k/→[t] in *tsha tsiok tsē* 'differ very much'; (d) innovative realization of /k/→[ʔ] in *kám-kak* 'to feel'; (e) total deletion of /k/ in *kok-gí* 'national language'.

tāi-hȧk ê sî-tsūn 'during college, lit. college GEN time', and Figure 17c is an example of anticipatory assimilation of /k/→[t] in *tsha tsiok tsē* 'differ very much'.

The "innovative" category refers to realizations not prescribed by any known phonological rule. For example, the final /k/ of *kám-kak* 'to feel' was realized as [ʔ] instead (Figure 17d). Since there is currently no phonological rule dictating such a change, it is operationally defined as an innovative form by the speaker. There are potentially two accounts underlying this type of realization. First, speakers might be unfamiliar with the exact realization of the final obstruent of the lexical item, and either mistook [kaʔ] as the pronunciation for /kak/ or used [ʔ] as a default replacement for all the coda obstruents of which they were unclear. Second, speakers might be starting a new process of further simplifying the system so that the oral gestures of the final /p t k/ are slowly eroding away, and only the glottal gesture that often accompanies oral stops remains. This is not unheard of. For example, Pó-chéng-uā, a related Min language spoken on a small outlying island of Wuqiu (see Figure 1), has undergone the erosion process of keeping only the final /ʔ/ but losing all the oral obstruents (Dai, 2007). There are also other types of innovative realizations besides realizing oral stops as [ʔ]. For example, an instance of /p/ in *--jȧp-khì* 'to enter' was found to be realized as [t] instead. Table 29 shows the distribution of the innovative usages in our data. Of the 428 instances of final obstruents collected, there were only 14 such tokens. However, they were not distributed evenly. There seemed to be a stronger tendency for the oral /p t k/ to be realized as [ʔ] than for them to be realized as other oral [p t k] options, especially in spontaneous speech. More importantly, there was no instance of /ʔ/→[p t k] that could not be explained by anticipatory assimilation. Regarding the predominance of /p t k/→[ʔ], it was unclear from the distribution which of these two accounts is more plausible. More studies are required in order to determine this.

Finally, the "deletion" category in Figure 16 refers to the total deletion of a coda obstruent that is not otherwise regulated by a phonological rule. This pertains to the realizations of the final /p t k/ and also the word-final /ʔ/, but not

Table 29 Innovative usages of final obstruents. /p t k/→[ʔ]: oral stops were realized as a glottal stop; /p t k/→[p t k]: oral stops were realized as another oral stop; "others" refers to a single case in which the change involved a nasal instead (/k/→[ŋ]).

	/p t k/→[ʔ]	/p t k/→[p t k]	Others
Read	2	1	---
Spontaneous	8	2	1

the word-medial /ʔ/. Although deletions in these positions all indicate a total loss of the final coda gesture, only the former two are not designated by a phonological rule, while the latter one is (see [6]). Therefore, the former two are included in this category, but the latter one is considered as one of the "regular" realizations of /ʔ/ instead. Figure 17e shows an example of the "deletion" category. The final /k/ in *kok-gí* 'national language' was completely deleted, resulting in an open syllable.

The distribution in Figure 16 is intriguing, as it shows at least two traits that do not exactly coincide with previous studies (cf. Chen, 2009b, 2010b; Pan & Lyu, 2021). First of all, /ʔ/ did not appear as eroding at the fastest pace in our data. In fact, it seemed fairly comparable to /t/ and /k/ in terms of its regular realizations. We suspect this discrepancy might be at least partly due to the adoption of different stimuli and categorization criteria. Chen (2009b, 2010b) studied word-final obstruent codas of monosyllabic and bisyllabic words in isolation (e.g., *káu-tsàp* 'ninty'), while Pan and Lyu (2021) examined word-medial obstruent codas of bisyllabic words in a carrier sentence (e.g., *Sing thiann sik-lāi ê siann-tiāu* 'First listen to the tone of *indoors*.'). To make our data a little more comparable, we first limited our observations to only prepausal /p t k/ tokens, which would be prosodically more similar to the isolated words in Chen (2009b, 2010b). Results are shown in the second column of Table 30, and the /ʔ/ deletion rate was indeed much higher than /k/ deletion (64% vs. 16%), while no deletion was found in this position for /p/ and /t/. Second, we limited our observations to only sentence-medial coda obstruents to be more comparable to the dataset used in Pan and Lyu (2021). Since they seemed to have treated all four obstruents equally, and did not take into consideration the word-internal deletion rule of /ʔ/, we also did the same with our data. Results are shown in the third column of Table 30. Again, the /ʔ/ deletion rate was much higher than the /t/ and /k/ deletion

Table 30 Distribution of coda obstruent deletion rates reorganized in ways more comparable to Chen (2009b, 2010b) (i.e., prepausal) and Pan & Lyu (2021) (i.e., sentence-medial). Numbers to the left of the "/" represent instances of deletion while those to the right represent total instances.

	Prepausal	Sentence-medial
/p/	0/13	0/19
/t/	0/5	30/100
/k/	11/67	12/55
/ʔ/	124/195	92/162

rates (57% vs. 30% vs. 22%), and there was no instance of deletion for /p/ in this position. This shows that if one does not take the phonological deletion rule of /ʔ/ into account, then /ʔ/ deletion is always more prevalent than that of /p t k/. However, this does not necessarily imply that /ʔ/ will disappear. As there was also a tendency for random tokens of /p t k/ to be realized as [ʔ] (Table 29), it is currently difficult to predict which of the final obstruents will disappear first.

The largest discrepancy regarding /ʔ/ between the current findings and previous studies actually lies in whether /ʔ/ deletion is tone-dependent. Previous studies suggested that /ʔ/ in Tone 8 is more prone to be deleted than that in Tone 4 (Chen, 2009b, 2010b; Pan & Lyu, 2021). However, this was not observed in our data. Figure 16b shows that the deletion rate was in fact higher in Tone 4 than in Tone 8. If phonologically allowed /ʔ/ deletion was also included in the calculation, then the overall deletion rate of /ʔ/ was 66 percent for Tone 4 and 70 percent for Tone 8. We suspect the discrepancy stemmed from different sampling methods. Unlike Chen (2009b, 2010b) and Pan and Lyu (2021), we did not have comparable sets for the two tones. In fact, our collection consisted of predominantly Tone 4 rather than Tone 8 tokens ($N = 210$ vs. 24). Therefore, studies with more balanced tokens from both tones would be needed in order to see whether a stable tone-dependency effect exists in /ʔ/ deletion.

The second interesting pattern illustrated in Figure 16 is the resilience of the final /p/. Of the twenty tokens collected, there was only one single instance of innovative realization, in which *--jip-khi* /dzip.kʰi/ was realized as [dzit.kʰi]. All the remaining realizations were either the orthodox [p] or [β], or [t k] due to anticipatory assimilation. In other words, there was no deletion at all. This implies that erosion for coda /p/ is progressing at most at a slow pace compared to the remaining /t k ʔ/. However, this was not mentioned in previous studies (cf. Chen, 2009b, 2010b; Pan & Lyu, 2021). We suspect that this might have something to do with the higher visibility of the oral gesture, as /p/ is the most visual of the four final obstruent codas. Since we had relatively few tokens of coda /p/ in our data, more research would be required in order to confirm the stability of /p/.

Previous studies showed that the realizations of final /p t k ʔ/ were substantially influenced by syllable position, dialect, and gender (Chang, 1989; Chen, 2009b, 2010b; Pan & Lyu, 2021). The discrepancies between the current data and the previous data suggest that speech genre probably also plays a role. It is thus safe to say that the final obstruents in Taiwanese are under a long-term process of erosion. However, the progression of individual obstruents is largely influenced by both linguistic and nonlinguistic factors. More studies at various future time points are required in order for us to have a clearer picture of this phenomenon.

5.5 Tone

To observe how base tones are realized in Taiwanese, syllables at utterance-final positions were examined. F0 measurements were taken from the voiced portions of these syllables (Howie, 1974), and Figure 18 shows the average realizations of the five smooth tones. There are three interesting observations.

First, although Taiwanese has two sets of tones that differ phonemically only in pitch register, Tone 1 and Tone 7, and Tone 2 and Tone 3, their acoustic realizations were not exactly comparable. For the pair of level tones, Tone 1 and Tone 7, both the F0 height and the F0 contour were somewhat different. Tone 1 was indeed higher than Tone 7 as prescribed, but only Tone 1 was relatively level. Tone 7 has a contour that is slightly dipping, and is closer to Tone 5. On the other hand, the pair of falling tones, Tone 2 and Tone 3, was more faithful to its phonemic prescriptions. Both were falling in contour and Tone 2 was consistently higher than Tone 3 regardless of genre and gender.

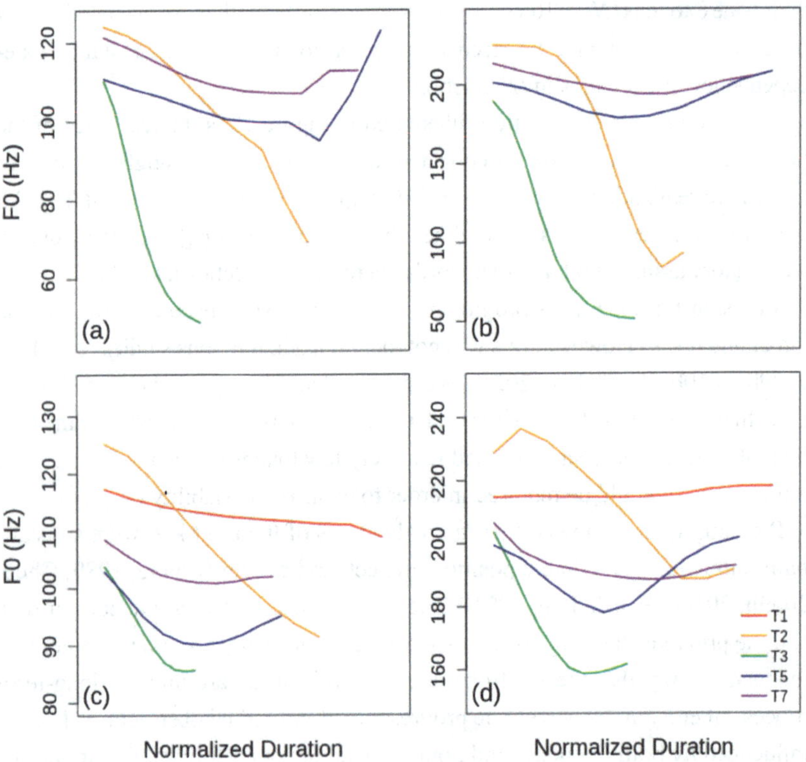

Figure 18 F0 excursions of the smooth tones in (a) male and (b) female read speech, and (c) male and (d) female spontaneous speech in utterance-final positions. There was no token of utterance-final Tone 1 in read speech.

Second, Tone 5 is acoustically found to be a dipping tone, even though it is phonologically deemed as rising. Across languages in the area, it is not uncommon to find rising tones to be realized with a slight initial fall. Both Taiwan and Mainland Mandarin show such a tendency (Fon & Chiang, 1999; Fon, Chiang & Cheung, 2004; Shi & Wang, 2006). The initial fall is considered a byproduct of the physiological effort required for achieving a rise, and is regarded as phonologically insignificant (Chao, 1956, 1968; Shih, 1988). However, perceptual experiments have shown that listeners do actively use the initial portion to help tonal detection when necessary (Fon et al., 2004). What strikes us as intriguing is the high resemblance in the realizations of the rising tones between Taiwanese and Taiwan Mandarin. Both tend to have their turning points situated around the center of the tone, and both have a shallow rise following a shallow fall. For both languages, the rising tone could at most be considered as a mid-rising tone. On the other hand, although Shi and Wang (2006) also showed a slight dipping contour for Mainland Mandarin, the turning point is fairly early, at around 20 percent of the tone. The rise is also a prominent one, and usually ends at the high end of the tonal range, making it a high-rising tone. Figure 19 shows a comparison of three bisyllabic words of rising tones in Taiwanese, Taiwan Mandarin, and Mainland Mandarin. It is clear from the figure that there is high resemblance in the realization of the rising tones between Taiwanese (Figure 19a) and Taiwan Mandarin (Figure 19b), while the rising tones in Mainland Mandarin are more dissimilar (Figure 19c). The pitch range of the rise is larger, and the initial falling portion is shorter (Fon & Chiang, 1999; Fon et al., 2004; Shi & Wang, 2006). This suggests that the resemblance between Taiwanese and Taiwan Mandarin is probably due to language contact, and the direction is more likely from Taiwanese to Mandarin than vice versa.

Finally, there were also some patterns in duration worth noting. In read speech, the rising Tone 5 was longer than the two falling tones, Tone 2 and Tone 3, though it was only longer than Tone 2 and not longer than Tone 3 in spontaneous speech (see Figure 18). This is in line with previous studies (Gandour, 1977; Yu, 2010). Moreover, the high-falling Tone 2 was always longer than the mid-falling Tone 3, probably because the mid-falling tone spanned a smaller F0 range and thus required less time to achieve the tonal targets. On the other hand, the duration difference between the high-level Tone 1 and the mid-level Tone 7 was quite intriguing, as it clearly violated observations from previous studies that vowel duration is inversely correlated with F0 (Gandour, 1977). We suspect this might have something to do with the acoustic realizations of the two aforementioned tones. As dynamic tones tend to be perceptually longer than static ones, it is possible that the mid-level Tone 7 is

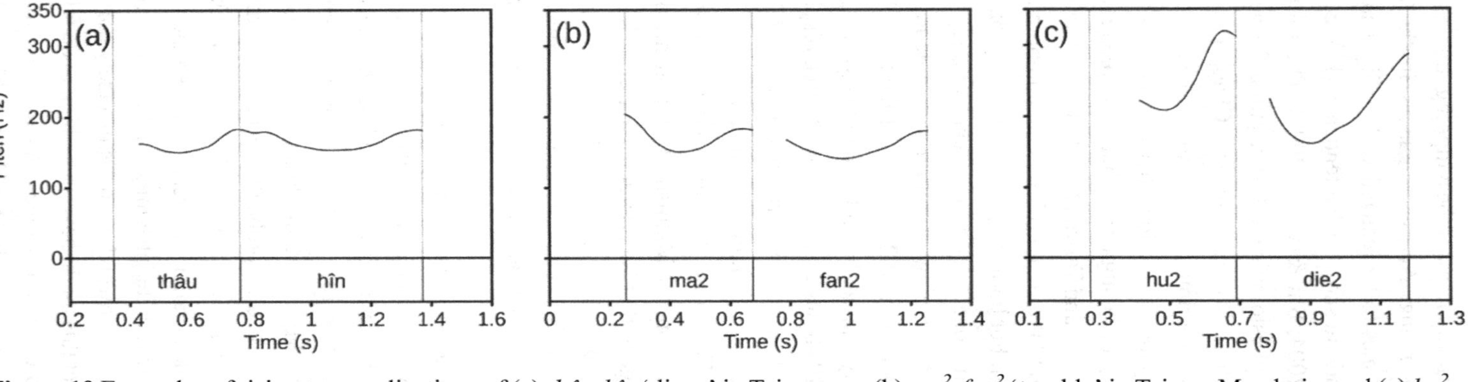

Figure 19 Examples of rising tone realizations of (a) *thâu-hîn* 'dizzy' in Taiwanese, (b) ma^2-fan^2 'trouble' in Taiwan Mandarin, and (c) hu^2-die^2 'butterfly' in Mainland Mandarin. (a) and (b) were recorded by the first author. (c) was taken from the soundtrack of a Youtube video (www.youtube.com/watch?v=enH-XW5kxKA).

Table 31 Distribution of the realizations of the checked tones in the utterance-final position. Underline indicates checked tones have lost their final obstruents.

	T4	**T8**
Read	T4: 75% T7: 25% ($n = 4$)	T4: 33% T7: 33% T8: 33% ($n = 3$)
Spontaneous	T4: 68% T8: 16% T1: 12% ($n = 25$)	T4: 86% T7: 14% ($n = 7$)
Spontaneous (*ah* excluded)	T4: 94% ($n = 18$)	---

perceptually licensed to be short. More studies are needed in order to observe the interplay between acoustic tonal realizations and their perceptual duration.

As for the checked tones, the realizations were much messier, especially for Tone 8. As shown in Table 31, we collected more tokens of utterance-final Tone 4 than Tone 8. Tone 4 tokens were predominantly realized as the canonical mid tone (Figure 20a). Tokens of Tone 4 being realized as either Tone 1 or Tone 8 were all contributed by the utterance-initial interjection *ah* 'well', which was always realized with a high-level contour. Therefore, if the final obstruent remained, then it became a Tone 8, and if it was deleted, then it became a Tone 1 (Figure 20b).

The realization of Tone 8 was even more varied. Of the ten tokens collected, only one was realized as the canonical high-falling tone (Figure 21a) (Chang, 1989). The majority were realized as a mid Tone 4 instead (Figure 21b). In other words, the base Tone 8 was to a large extent merged with the base Tone 4. When the final obstruent was eradicated, the tone became a mid-level Tone 7 (Figure 21c). This suggests that Taiwanese is probably undergoing a simplifying process in terms of its checked base tones, and is gradually moving from a seven-tone system to a six-tone one. This is consistent with Chen's (2009b, 2010b) observations and predictions.

5.6 Syllable Fusion

Syllable fusion is a common phenomenon in Taiwanese. Table 32 shows the words that were fused multiple times in the corpus. Almost all fused instances were originally bisyllabic. The fused form of *tsha-put-to* 'about' was the only one that was trisyllabic. At the segmental level, most fusion followed the edge-in rule

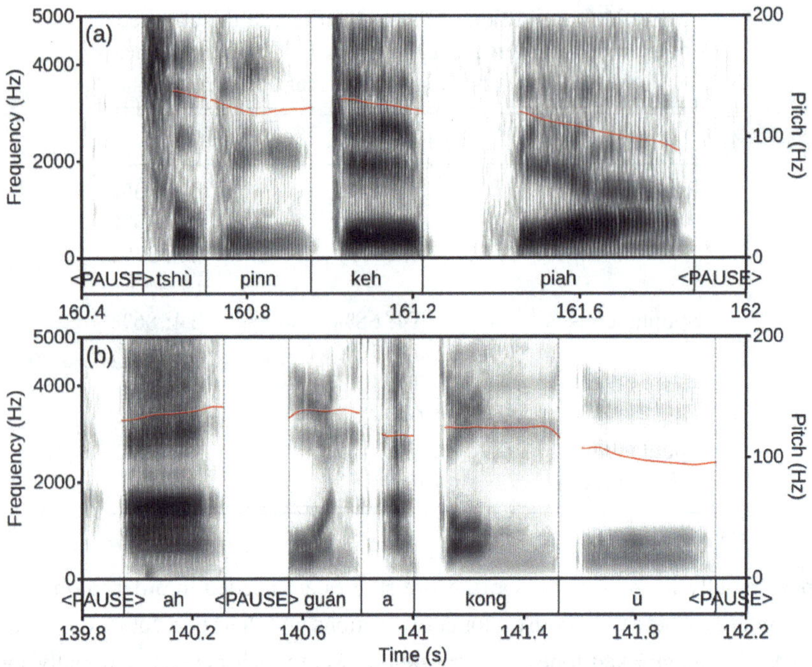

Figure 20 The base Tone 4 being realized as (a) the canonical mid-falling Tone 4 *piah* in *tshù-pinn-keh-**piah*** 'neighbors'; (b) the high-level Tone 8 *ah* in ***ah*** *guán a-kong ū* 'well, my grandfather has … '

and the L-R-scanning rule (Chung, 1996) (see Section 2.4.4). According to these two rules, the fused forms of *khng* [kʰŋ̩] and *iunn* [ĩũ] for *khó-lîng* 'possibly' and *in-uī* 'because', respectively, would be considered exceptions. The former chose [ŋ] over [ə] for the vowel nucleus, violating the L-R-scanning rule and the vocoid association rule, while the latter chose the [u] over [i] from the second syllable, violating the edge-in rule.

At the tonal level, the edge-in principle was even more likely to be violated. From Table 32, it is clear that the first tonal target of the first syllable seemed to have priority and was always chosen to be in the fused form. However, the target chosen seemed somewhat less predictable for the second syllable. In some cases, the first target was chosen, as in *bô ài* 'do not want' and *in-uī* 'because'; in other cases, the second target was chosen, as in *sóo-í* 'so' (Figure 22). The fused form of the trisyllabic word *tsha-put-to* 'about' was an even clearer blatant violation of the rule, as it was the tonal target from the second syllable that was chosen, not the third. More importantly, the fused form was found in three different speakers (M4, F3, and F4), so it could not be easily explained as idiosyncratic pronunciation.

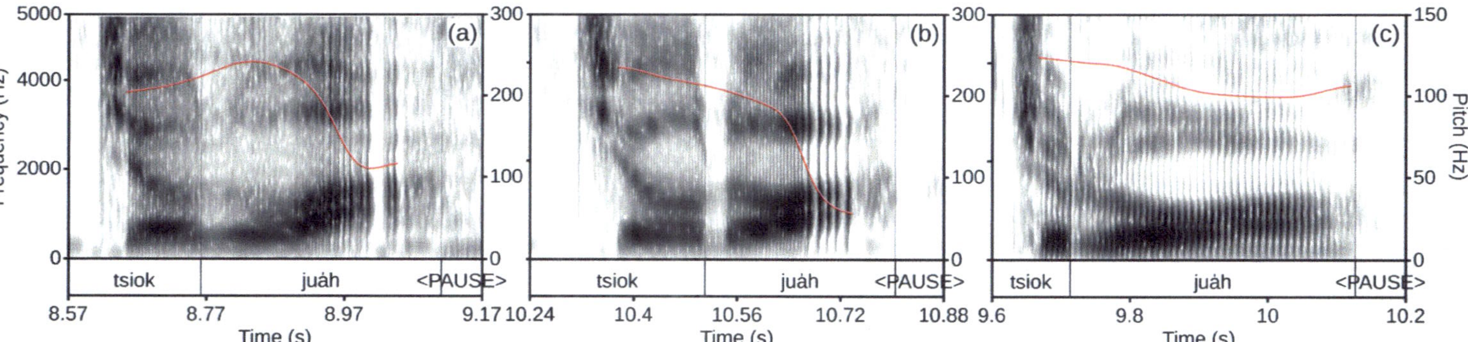

Figure 21 The base Tone 8 being realized as (a) the canonical high-falling Tone 8, (b) the mid-falling Tone 8, and the mid-level Tone 7 for *juàh* in *tsiok **juàh*** 'very hot'.

Table 32 Syllable fusion with multiple instances. Underline indicates words that ended in a sandhi form. Tonal targets are in parentheses. Red indicates influences from the first syllable, green indicates influences from the middle syllable, blue indicates influences from the last syllable, and purple indicates influences from both the first and the last syllables.

Phrase/word	Fused form	Gloss	N
(a) Read			
bô ài	*buai*	'do not want'	3
(MM+HM)	(MH)		
(b) Spontaneous			
khó-lîng	*khong* (*n* = 3)	'possibly'	5
(HH+MM)	*khng* (*n* = 2)		
	(HM)		
tsha-put-to	*tshao* (*n* = 1)	'about'	4
(MM+H+MM)	*tshiao* (*n* = 3)		
	(MH)		
sóo-í	*sue*	'so'	4
(HH+HM)	(HM)		
kám-kak	*kann*	'to feel'	3
(HH+H)	(HH)		
in-uī	*iunn*	'because'	2
(MM+ML)	(MM)		
--khí-lâi	*--khai*	'start to'	2
(LL+LL)	(LL)		
kā lâng	*kang*	'to people'	2
(ML+MM)	(ML) (*n* = 1)		
	(MM) (*n* = 1)		
tī-leh	*te*	'at'	2
(ML-H)	(MH)		

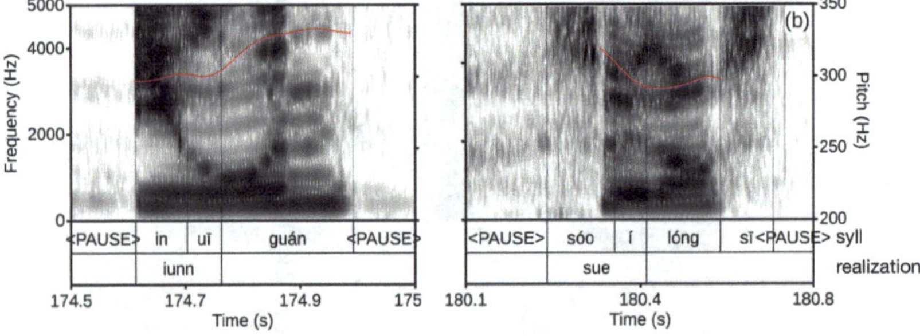

Figure 22 Syllable fusion in (a) *in-uī* 'because' and (b) *sóo-í* 'so'.

5.7 Prosodic Hierarchy

As a tone language, Taiwanese probably imposes a greater restriction on how prosodic tunes can vary, much like Mandarin (Peng et al., 2005) and Cantonese (Wong et al., 2005). However, this does not imply the total absence of prosody in Taiwanese, but instead, an intricate interaction between tone and prosodic tunes is in action. We followed Peng and Beckman's (2003) system and labeled Tone 2 and Tone 5 at both IP- and TSG-final positions (Figure 23). As both tones span a substantial tonal range, one could thus observe how pitch range in prosody interacts with tonal register and tonal range. One could also examine whether tonal contours are preserved under the effect of declination. As shown in the figure, the overall tonal contour was not different at the two prosodic levels for the high-falling Tone 2. Both were realized as falling. However, the degree of the fall was much larger before IP than TSG boundaries, and the difference was larger in read than spontaneous speech. In addition, TSG-final Tone 2 started at a much higher register than those before IP boundaries in read speech, while not much difference was found in spontaneous speech. This suggests that final lowering was indeed more prominent in the IP-final position for T2, but the effect was stronger in read speech, exerting an influence on both the initial tonal register and the final fall. In spontaneous speech, the effect was more obvious in the final fall only. There was also a substantial difference in duration between the two prosodic levels. Regardless of speech genre, IP-final Tone 2 was consistently longer than TSG-final Tone 2, indicating a stronger final lengthening effect at higher prosodic boundaries. This was generally in line with previous studies (Kuo, 2011, 2012; Pan & Tai, 2006; Peng, 1997).

Although previous studies only looked at the falling Tone 2, we also included the other contour tone in Taiwanese, the rising Tone 5. Because the second half of the tonal contour goes against the direction of declination, it would be interesting to see how they interact. As shown in Figure 23, the typical dipping contour of Tone 5 was only well preserved in IP-final position. In TSG-final position, only female spontaneous speech showed such a contour. For male spontaneous speech and female read speech, only the initial fall was observed, but not the final rise. For male read speech, even the initial fall was not realized, and the contour became flat. In other words, within the same genre, females were generally more conservative for contour preservation than males. For Tone 5 tokens realized with the initial falling and/or the final rising portion, the IP-final position showed a larger excursion, but the difference was not as large as that in Tone 2, probably because of the intrinsic physiological constraint of the tone (Shi & Wang, 2006), and conflict between the tonal contour and the declination trend. There was not much difference in the initial tonal register

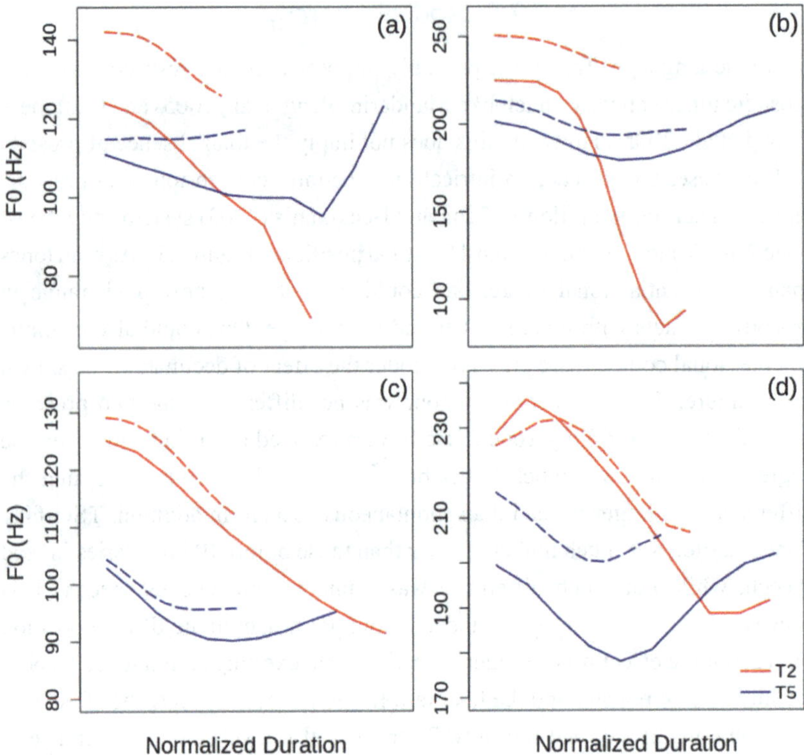

Figure 23 Average tonal excursions of Tone 2 and Tone 5 at IP- and TSG-final positions in (a) male and (b) female read speech, and (c) male and (d) female spontaneous speech. Solid lines are tones at IP boundaries and dashed lines are tones at TSG boundaries.

between IP- and TSG-final positions either. Except for female spontaneous speech (Figure 23d), which showed a large difference, Tone 5 tokens at these two prosodic levels began at about the same tonal register. This shows that final lowering did not exert a differential effect on the realization of Tone 5 at the two prosodic levels.

Comparing Tone 2 and Tone 5 across different prosodic positions and speech genres suggested that the effect that prosodic tunes and pitch range impose on tones at prosodic boundaries is likely dependent on a variety of factors. In general, tonal contours are preserved better at large prosodic boundaries than smaller ones, in falling tones than rising ones, in spontaneous speech than read speech, and among females than males. This implies that linguistic, sociolinguistic, and physiological factors might all be involved in Taiwanese prosody. More studies would be needed in order to understand the strength of these factors and how they interact.

6 Future Research

Looking across research on Taiwanese, one finds at least two areas that are especially lacking. The first is prosody. Although Peng and Beckman (2003) have sketched out a rough prosodic structure for Taiwanese, very little has been done to test how the model could be refined or modified. The majority of research on Taiwanese still focuses on segmental and tonal variations across dialects only. This is unfortunate, as Taiwanese provides a perfect testing ground for examining interactions among tone, stress, rhythm, and prosody. Compared to Mandarin, it has a richer tone inventory, a more robust stress system, and a more varied syllable structure, in addition to a tone sandhi rule set that is far more intricate and sensitive to suprasegmental elements. It would thus be theoretically interesting to see how prosody could be instantiated in such a complex system.

The other area that is often lacking is a cognitive perspective on how learners and speakers process such a system. Because of the switch from a Taiwanese-dominant to a Mandarin-dominant society due to the Mandarin-only policy (Huang, 1993; Lin, 2001), the research stance regarding the age factor is often from the point of language decay and language loss. Younger speakers are regularly regarded as losing ground in Taiwanese due to insufficient proficiency through processes such as simplification, lenition, and deletion. While the decline of Taiwanese usage and proficiency in the younger generations is true, such a perspective will not be of much help in revitalizing the language itself. More studies on how a weaker language is acquired and processed would be extremely helpful for the younger speakers today to develop a full Taiwanese system and for the language to regain its vitality in the society as a whole. The future awaits, but its brightness depends largely on what we do today.

Appendix

What follows are the transcripts of the Taiwanese recording excerpts from the Mandarin-Taiwanese Spontaneous Speech Corpus (Fon, 2004) in both the standard character system and the romanization system of M3, M4, F3, and F4. English translation is also provided to facilitate understanding. Both of the female speakers co-switched to Mandarin several times in their excerpts. As Mandarin is the dominant and official language in Taiwan, this is a fairly common phenomenon. Mandarin utterances are indicated through underline, and its romanization follows the Hanyu pinyin system. To protect the speakers' privacy, their names were edited out.

M3

Q: 好，敢會當請你先介紹你家己？
Hó, kám ē-tàng tshiánn lí sing kài-siāu lí ka-kī?
Okay, can you please first introduce yourself?

A: 我叫 XXX。Honnh。X是XX的X，X是XXXX的X。
Guá kiò XXX. Honnh. X sī XX ê X, X sī XXXX ê X.
My name is XXX. Yeah. X is the X of XX, X is the X of XXXX.

Q: 喔，好。啊蹛佇佗位啊？
Oh hó. Ah tuà tī tó-uī--ah?
Oh, okay. And where do you live?

A: 我蹛佇台中縣清水。
Guá tuà tī Tâi-tiong-kuān Tshing-tsuí.
I live in Tshing-tsuí in Tâi-tiong County.

Q: 今年幾歲啊？
Kin-nî kuí huè--ah?
How old are you this year?

A: 今年三十三歲。
Kin-nî sann-tsàp-sann huè.
I am thirty-three this year.

Q: 三十三囉。喔，按呢算算講對清水遮非常了解就著矣。
Sann-tsàp-sann--looh. Ooh, án-ne sǹg sǹg kóng tuì Tshing-tsuí tsia hui-siông liáu-kái tō tiòh--ah.
Already thirty-three. Oh, that means you should be very familiar with Tshing-tsuí.

A: Unn 講了解是無啦，但是就佇遮蹛三十幾年矣。
Unn kóng liáu-kái sī bô lah, tān-sī tō tī tsia tuà sann-tsàp kuí nî--ah.
Um, I would not say I am familiar, but I have lived here for thirty-some years.

Q: 好。所以遮會當請你講看覓仔的，以前的清水含這馬有啥物無仝？
Hó. Sóo-í tsia ē-tàng tshiánn lí kóng-khuànn-māi-á--ê, í-tsîng ê Tshing-tsuí hām tsit-má ū siánn-mih bô kāng?
Okay. So can you please talk a little bit about how Tshing-tsuí now is different from before?

A: 以前的清水喔，喔，我會記得以前的清水。若阮蹛的遮，這個所在--honnh, 叫武鹿。以前做囡仔的時陣的武鹿農田較濟。然後就是迌迌攏佇田的嘛。啊，這馬，路嘛足細條，而且攏田岸仔路。啊這馬的武鹿這個所在就著啊啦，就是路攏開足大條的，啊田嘛愈愈愈少啊。啊以前佇田的耍，這馬的囡仔應該是攏無佇田的耍矣。啊若清水來講，以前的清水，較鬧熱。啊這馬的清水可能人口漸漸攏出去外口矣--honnh, 所以清水的感覺就無像以前遐鬧熱矣。
Í-tsîng ê Tshing-tsuí--ooh, ooh, guá ē kì-tit í-tsîng ê Tshing-tsuí. Nā guán tuà ê tsia, tsit-ê sóo-tsāi--honnh, kiò Bú-lòk. Í-tsîng tsò gín-á ê sî-tsūn ê Bú-lòk lông-tshân khah tsē. Jiân-āu tō sī tshit-thô lóng tī tshân--ê--mah. Ah, tsit-má, lōo mā tsiok sè tiâu, jî-tshiánn lóng tshân-huānn-á-lōo. Ah tsit-má ê Bú-lòk tsit-ê sóo-tsāi tō tiòh--ah--lah, tō sī lōo lóng khui tsiok tuā tiâu--ê, ah tshân mā jú jú jú tsió--ah. Ah í-tsîng tī tshân--ê sńg, tsit má ê gín-á ing-kai sī lóng bô tī tshân--ê sńg--ah. Ah nā Tshing-tsuí lâi kóng, í-tsîng ê Tshing-tsuí, khah lāu-jiàt. Ah tsit-má ê Tshing-tsuí khó-lîng jîn-kháu tsiām-tsiām lóng tshut-khì guā-kháu--ah--honnh, sóo-í Tshing-tsuí ê kám-kak tō bô tshiūnn í-tsîng hiah lāu-jiàt--ah.
Tshing-tsuí from before? Oh, I remember what it was like before in Tshing-tsuí. If we are talking about the place we are living here, this place, it's called Bú-lòk. When I was a kid, there were more fields in Bú-lòk. And we all played in the fields. And, now, the roads used to be very narrow, and they were all field paths. And now, this place of Bú-lòk, the roads are very wide, and there are fewer and fewer fields. And we used to play in the fields, but kids nowadays likely do not have any fields to play in. And as for Tshing-tsuí, Tshing-tsuí used to be busier. And I think people now have probably gradually moved out of Tshing-tsuí, so I feel that Tshing-tsuí is not as busy as before.

Q: 所以武鹿這個所所在算是較庄腳嗎？
Sóo-í Bú-lòk tsit-ê sóo- sóo-tsāi sǹg sī khah tsng-kha--ma?
So this p- place of Bú-lòk counts as more rural?

A: Unn 遮，遮應該算較庄跤一寡。
Unn, tsia, tsia ing-kai sǹg khah tsng-kha--tsit-kuá.
Um, this place, this place should be counted as a bit more rural.

Q: 所以像人情味咧?敢有改變?
Sóo-í tshiūnn jîn-tsîng-bī--leh? Kám ū kái-piàn?
And how about the human touch? Has it changed?

A: 人情味喔?人情味佇遮來講應該，unn參以前比起來應該是有啦。因為
   這馬人口啊，啥s, unn嘛是加加減減無像以前較有人情味。但是這馬
   嘛袂講差足濟的，因為大家厝邊隔壁，大家攏蹛一二十年矣。基本
   上攏是老厝邊矣，所以感覺起來是差不多啦。Hm。

   Jîn-tsîng-bī--ooh? Jîn-tsîng-bī tī tsia lâi kóng ing-kai, unn tsham í-tsîng pí--khí-lâi ing-kai sī ū--lah. In-uī tsit-má jîn-kháu--ah, siánn s, unn mā sī ke-ke-kiám-kiám bô tshiūnn í-tsîng khah ū jîn-tsîng-bī. Tān-sī tsit-má mā bē kóng tsha tsiok tsē--ê, in-uī tak-ke tshù-pinn-keh-piah, tak-ke lóng tuà it-jī-tsap nî--ah. Ki-pún-siōng lóng sī lāu tshù-pinn--ah, sóo-í kám-kak--khí-lâi sī tsha-put-to--lah. Hm.

   Human touch? The human touch here should, um, compared to before, have
   changed. Because of the population now, s-, um, the human touch is somewhat
   not as much as before. But there is not that much difference either because
   everyone lives close by, and all of us have lived here for ten, twenty years.
   Basically we have been neighbors for a long time, so it feels about the same.
   Hm.

Q: 啊像以前彼含恁鬥陣的朋友啊，做伙讀國校的國中的，大部份佇咧
   這馬敢閣有咧聯絡?

   Ah tshiūnn í-tsîng he hām lín tàu-tīn ê pîng-iú--ah, tsò-hué thak kok-hāu--ê kok-tiong--ê, tuā-pōo-hūn tī teh tsit-má kám koh ū teh liân-lòk?

   And how about the friends you used to hang out with, those going to the
   same elementary school and middle school? Do you still get in touch with
   most of them?

A: 國校國中，有啊，嘛是攏有咧聯絡啊。啊攏蹛佇附近啊。出門有當時
   仔就去踅一下夜市仔的，踅過去去街仔，去佗位啊，有當時仔攏會抵
   著啊。

   Kok hāu kok tiong, ū--ah, mā sī lóng ū teh liân lòk--ah. Ah lóng tuà tī hù-kīn--ah. Tshut-mn̂g ū-tang-sî-á tō khì sèh tsit-ē iā-tshī-á--ê, sèh kuè-khì khì ke-á, khì tó uī--ah, ū-tang-sî-á lóng ē tú--tioh--ah.

   Elementary school and middle school, yes, we still get in touch with each other.
   And they all live nearby. Sometimes when I go out to visit the night market, or
   go shopping, or go somewhere, we will sometimes run into each other.

M4

Q: 好，unn請你先介紹你家己。
   Hó, unn tshiánn lí sing kài-siāu lí ka-kī.
   Okay, um, please first introduce yourself.

A: 我，我叫XXX。啊我是台中人。阮兜佇台中，龍井。啊阮兜遐，你嘛
   會使講阮兜遐另外一个名叫茄投。但是阮兜就是台中縣龍井鄉。啊阮
   彼个所在人攏，是田中村啦。但是人嘛會使講彼个所在，因為阮隔壁

庄的，彼幾个仔所在，逐家攏，以早人古早人攏講，喔，遐叫做, enn
茄投。所以若是外口人, 毋知影講茄投是啥物所在。因為你你你若看
住址, 無茄投這个名。啊你若講, unn你若講是台中遐的人，阮台中縣
海線遐的人，你共人講，人才知。啊你若講毋是毋是遐的人honn, 你
共人講茄投，無人知，因為彼住址無無寫彼彼款名。啊阮攏是按呢講
啦。阮攏是茄投遐的人。Henn。啊阮兜佇較倚海邊仔。阮阮台中，
阮，線, uh算海線的嘛。台中縣有分山線佮海線。山線就是豐原、台
中、苗栗彼爿。啊阮兜是清水、沙鹿、梧棲、龍井、大肚這爿，所以
阮這爿是海線--ê。啊阮兜佇龍井這爿遮，所以較倚海邊仔, henn, 倚台
中港遐。啊阮兜就，阮自，阮阮阮姓陳嘛。啊阮兜差不多佇遐一兩
百，差不多兩百年有喔。Henn。因為阮算算算足久的，算足久的攏佇
遐，攏佇彼个所在。自對對大陸彼爿過來，就一直佇遮。Henn。啊算
算講祖唇嘛攏佇遮，所以阮攏佇遮。啊我嘛佇遮大漢的。啊阮阿公，
阮叫，阮姓陳。但是你若講姓陳的，有足濟。有啥物陳四德。啊阮是
陳三公，三公。我嘛毋知是按怎叫陳三公。但是阮遐有另外一庄叫陳
四德。阮是雖然講攏姓陳，但是無啥仝。Henn。啊阮阿公有有幾个兄
弟我毋知，因為有的已經過身去矣。啊我有，我想看覓，有有兩个阿
伯，有三个阿叔，但是, eh?Huan, henn, 有三个阿叔。啊thōng細漢彼个
阿叔自, thōng, 自一出生就予分人矣，但是阮這馬閣有聯絡啦。啊但是
伊嘛是姓陳，因為伊分人彼个彼彼彼家伙仔嘛是仝款姓陳。但是就是
毋是毋是，這馬阮無做伙矣，但是猶有聯絡。啊另外兩个阿叔攏已經
過身去矣。一个阿叔咧做兵的時陣，就過身去矣。毋知。講是佇外
島。毋知按怎，就就就死去矣。

*Guá, guá kiò XXX. Ah guá sī Tâi-tiong lâng. Guán tau tī Tâi-tiong, Liông-
tsénn. Ah guán tau hia, lí mā ē-sái kóng guán tau hia līng-guā tsit ê miâ kiò Ka-
tâu. Tān-sī guán tau tō sī Tâi-tiong-kuān Liông-tsénn-hiong. Ah guán hit ê sóo-
tsāi lâng lóng, sī Tiân-tiong-tshuan--lah. Tān-sī lâng mā ē-sái kóng hit ê sóo-
tsāi, in-uī guán keh-piah tsng--ê, he kuí-ê-á sóo-tsāi, tȧk ke lóng, í-tsá-lâng
kóo-tsá-lâng lóng kóng, ooh, hia kiò tsò, enn Ka-tâu. Sóo-í nā sī guā-kháu-
lâng, m̄ tsai-iánn kóng Ka-tâu sī siánn-mih sóo-tsāi. In-uī lí lí lí nā khuànn tsū-
tsí, bô Ka-tâu tsit ê miâ. Ah lí nā kóng, unn lí nā kóng sī Tâi-tiong hia ê lâng,
guán Tâi-tiong-kuān Hái-suànn hia ê lâng, lí kā lâng kóng, lâng tsiah tsai. Ah lí
nā kóng m̄ sī m̄ sī hia ê lâng honn, lí kā lâng kóng Ka-tâu, bô lâng tsai, in-uī he
tsū-tsí bô bô siá hit hit khuán miâ. Ah guán lóng sī án-ne kóng--lah. Guán lóng
sī Ka-tâu hia ê lâng. Henn. Ah guán tau tī khah uá hái-pinn-á. Guán guán Tâi-
tiong, guán, suànn, uh sǹg Hái-suànn--ê--mah. Tâi-tiong-kuān ū hun Suann-
suànn kah Hái-suànn. Suann-suànn tō sī Hong-guân, Tâi-tiong, Biâu-lȧk hit
pîng. Ah guán tau sī Tshing-tsuí, Sua-lak, Gôo-tshe, Liông-tsénn, Tuā-tōo tsit
peng, sóo-í guán tsit pîng sī Hái-suànn--ê. Ah guán tau tī Liông-tsénn tsit pîng
tsiah, sóo-í khah uá hái-pinn-á, henn, uá Tâi-tiong-káng hia. Ah guán tau tō,*

guán tsū, guán guán guán sènn Tân--mah. Ah guán tau tsha-put-to tī hia it-nñg-pah, tsha-put-to nñg-pah nî ū--ooh. Henn. in-uī guán sǹg sǹg sǹg tsiok kú--ê, sǹg tsiok kú--ê lóng tī hia, lóng tī hit ê sóo-tsāi. Tsū tuì tuì Tāi-liòk hit pîng kuè--lâi, tō it-tı̍t tī tsia. Henn. Ah sǹg sǹg kóng tsóo-tshù mā lóng tī tsia, sóo-í guán lóng tī tsia. Ah guá mā tī tsia tuā-hàn--ê. Ah guán a-kong, guán kiò, guán sènn Tân. Tān-si lí nā kóng sènn Tân--ê, ū tsiok tsē. Ū siann-mih Tân Sù-tik. Ah guán sī Tân Sam-kong, Sam-kong. Guá mā m̄ tsai sī-án-tsuánn kiò Tân Sam-kong. Tān-sī guán hia ū līng-guā tsı̍t tsng in kiò Tân Sù-tik. Guán sī sui-jiân kóng lóng sènn Tân, tān-sī bô siánn kâng. Henn. Ah guán a-kong ū ū kuí ê hiann-tī guá m̄ tsai, in-uī ū ê í-king kuè-sin--khì--ah. Ah guá ū, guá siūnn khuànn-māi, ū ū nñg ê a-peh ū sann ê a-tsik, tān-sī, eh? Huan, henn, ū sann ê a-tsik. Ah thōng sè-hàn hit ê a-tsik tsū, thōng, tsū tsı̍t tshut-senn tō hōo pun--lâng--ah, tān-sī guán tsit-má kok ū liân-lòk--lah. Ah tān-sī i mā sī sènn Tân, in-uī i pun--lâng hit ê hit hit hit ke-hué-á mā sī kāng-khuán sènn Tân. Tān sī tō sī m̄ sī m̄ sī, tsit-má guán bô tsò-huê--ah, tān-sī iáu ū liân-lòk. Ah līng-guā nñg ê a-tsik lóng í-king kuè-sin--khì--ah. Tsı̍t ê a-tsik teh tsò-ping ê sî-tsūn tō kuè-sin--khì--ah. M̄ tsai. Kóng sī tī guā-tó. M̄ tsai án-tsuánn tō tō tō sí--khì--ah.

My, my name is XXX. And I am from Tâi-tiong. My hometown is Liông-tsénn, Tâi-tiong. As for my hometown, you can also say that my hometown has another name called Ka-tâu. But my hometown is Liông-tsénn Township, Tâi-tiong County. And the people in my hometown all, it is Tiân-tiong Village. But people also can call that place, because our neighboring villages, places around there, everyone all, people since the old days all said, oh, that place is called, um, Ka-tâu. So for people outside the area, they do not know where Ka-tâu is. Because if you you you check the address, there is no place called Ka-tâu. But if people are, um, if people are from Tâi-tiong, from our coastal area in Tâi-tiong, you say that, people will know. But if people are not not from that area, and you say Ka-tâu, no one knows because the address does not not use that name. But we all say it this way. We are all from Ka-tâu. Yeah. And my hometown is closer to the coast. We we Tâi-tiong, we, the area, uh, counts as the coastal area. Tâi-tiong County is divided into the mountainous area and the coastal area. The mountainous area includes places like Hong-guân, Tâi-tiong, and Biâu-lı̍k. And my hometown is in the area along Tshing-tsuí, Sua-lak, Gôo-tshe, Liông-tsénn, and Tuā-tōo, and so our place is the coastal area. And my hometown is in the Liông-tsénn area, so it is closer to the coast, yeah, near Tâi-tiong Harbor. My hometown, we since, our our our family name is Tân. My family has been here for approximately one, two hundred, approximately two hundred years. Yeah. Because we have been there for a very long, very long time, always at that place. Since we moved from from the Mainland, we have been living here. Yeah. And our ancestral home is also here, so we all live here. And I also grew up here. And my grandpa, we are called, our family name is Tân. But if you talk about the Tân families, there are many. For example, there is this Tân Sù-tik. And we are Tân Sam-kong, Sam-kong. I don't know why we are called Tân Sam-kong. But we have another village there called Tân Sù-tik. Although our family names are both Tân, we are not exactly the same. Yeah. And I don't know how many brothers my grandpa has because some have already passed away. And I have, let me think, have have two uncles older than my dad, and three uncles younger, but, eh? I, yeah, I have three uncles younger than my dad. And the youngest uncle was put up for adoption since since birth, but we still get in touch. But he also bears the family name of Tân because his foster family also has the last name of Tân. But it's not not, we do not live together now, but we still get in touch. The other two uncles younger than my dad already passed away. One uncle passed away when he was in the military. I don't know why. People said he was on an offshore island. I don't know what happened, but but but he died.

F3

Q: 好，enn 敢會使請你先介紹你家己?
Hó, enn kám ē-sái tshiánn lí sing kài-siāu lí ka-kī?
Okay, um, can you please first introduce yourself?

A: 喔，我叫XXX。然後我本來是蹛佇咧東勢，unn台中的東勢。啊就是，結果以後阮搬去豐原。然後才閣um後來搬去豐原，然後才閣搬去潭子。啊這馬是蹛佇咧台中市區附近遐。啊我是一個unn，我感覺算講是足愛講話的人吧。Mm可能自細漢阮兜做生理。就是阮兜是咧開鞋仔店，所以我較佮意佮人講話啊。然後較無法度，較無法，無法度按呢恬恬攏莫講話啊。所以阮媽媽攏感覺我足活潑的按呢啊。
Ooh, guá kiò XXX. Ran2-hou4 guá pún-lâi sī tuà tī-leh Tang-sì, unn Tâi-tiong ê Tang-sì. Ah tō sī, kiat-kó í-āu guán puann-khì Hong-guân. Ran2-hou4 tsiah koh um āu--lâi puann-khì Hong-guân, ran2-hou4 chiah koh poann-khì Tham-tsú. Ah tsit-má sī tuà tī-teh Tâi-tiong tshī-khu hù-kīn hia. Ah guá sī tsit ê unn, guá kám-kak sng-kóng sī tsiok ài kóng-uē ê lâng pah. Mm khó-lîng tsū sè-hàn guán tau tsò-seng-lí. Tō sī guán tau sī teh khui ê-á-tiàm, sóo-í guá khah kah-ì kah lâng kóng-uē--ah. Ran2-hou4 khah bô-hoat-tōo, khah bô-hoat, bô-hoat-tōo án-ne tiām-tiām lóng mài kóng-uē--ah. Sóo-í guán má-mah lóng kám-kak guá tsiok huàt-phuat--ê án-ne--ah.

Oh, my name is XXX. And originally I lived in Tang-sì, um Tang-sì in Tâi-tiong. And then later we moved to Hong-guân, and then moved to Tham-tsú. And now we live near Tâi-tiong City. And I am a, um, I feel I count as a talkative person. Mm maybe because my family has been running a business since I was a kid. My family opens a shoe store, so I like to talk to people more. And I cannot, cannot, cannot be quiet and not talk. So my mom always thinks I am very active.

Q: 啊你講你厝的做生理開店honn。啊你敢有捌鬥顧店？
Ah lí kóng lí tshù--ê tsò-sing-lí khui-tiàm honn. Ah lí kám ū bat tàu-kòo-tiàm?
And you said your family owns a business and opens a shop, right? And have you ever helped in the shop?

A: 有啊。我攏鬥顧店啊。就是可能上課下課轉來，就愛顧一个仔店啊。有人客來，就愛共伊招呼一下按呢。
Ū--ah. Guá lóng tàu-kòo-tiàm--ah. Tō sī khó-lîng siōng-khò hā-khò tńg-lâi, tō ài kòo tsit-ê-á tiàm--ah. Ū lâng-kheh lâi, tō ài kā i tsio-hoo--tsit-ē án-ne.
Yes. I have helped in the shop. Usually when I come back after school, I have to help a bit. If guests come, I will have to serve them.

Q: 若按呢顧店攏，差不多，你敢會，敢抵著懊客？
Nā án-ne kòo-tiàm lóng, tsha-put-to, lí kám ē, kám tú-tiòh àu-kheh?
When you help in the shop, about, have you ever, have you ever met difficult customers?

A: 懊客喔。其實懊客攏毋是我咧處理。懊客攏是阮爸爸媽媽咧處理。我只是就是看一下按呢。啊若是有人客欲揣鞋仔，幫伊揣一下按呢爾。懊客我是無啥物感覺。
Àu-kheh--ooh. Kî-sit àu-kheh lóng m̄ sī guá teh tshú-lí. Àu-kheh lóng sī guán pá-pah má-mah teh tshú-lí. Guá tsí-sī tō sī khuànn--tsit-ē án-ne. Ah nā sī ū lâng-kheh beh tshuē ê-á, pang i tshuē--tsit-ē án-ne niâ. Àu-kheh guá sī bô siánn-mih kám-kak.
Difficult customers. Actually, I don't need to deal with difficult customers at all. Usually my parents have to deal with them. I only sort of help around. And if a customer wants to find a certain pair of shoes, I will help him. That's it. I don't know much about difficult customers.

Q: 啊你捌聽過無？
Ah lí bat thiann--kuè--bô?
Have you ever heard of them before?

A: 有啊。其實我我家己佇今年的，enn今年過年我嘛有去彼打工。我嘛是去鞋仔店打工。但是，我家己去鞋仔店打工，我才知影真的是ts-真的是足濟懊客的。就是，就是去共你，去共你試穿。穿穿咧。然後試穿，穿一雙。然後穿穿咧，無佮意，閣換一雙。啊結果就差不多穿四五雙，結果攏無買，就走矣。然後就是裝痟的。
Ū--ah. Kî-sit guá guá ka-kī tī kin-nî ê, enn kin-nî kuè-nî guá mā ū khì he da3-gong1. Guá mā sī khì ê-á-tiàm da3-gong1. Tān-sī, guá ka-kī khì ê-á-tiàm da3-gong1, guá tsiah tsai-iánn tsin--ê sī ts- tsin--ê sī tsiok tsē àu-kheh--ê. Tō sī, tō sī khì kā lí, khì kā lí tshì tshīng. Tshīng-tshīng--leh. Ran2-hou4 tshì tshīng, tshīng tsit siang. Ran2-hou4 tshīng-tshīng--leh, bô kah-ì, koh uānn tsit siang. Ah kiat-kó tō tsha-put-to tshīng sì gōo siang, kiat-kó lóng bô bé, tō tsáu--ah. Ran2-hou4 tō sī tsng-siáu--ê.

Yes. Actually, I also worked part-time this year, um, this past Chinese New Year. I also worked at a shoe shop. But it is only after I went to work part-time at this shoe shop that I realized there ts- are really many difficult customers. They will just, just try out shoes with, with you. They try them out. And they try out, try out one pair. Then they try it out, they don't like it, and they switch to another pair. In the end, they will try out about four or five pairs, they will not buy any of them in the end, and then they will leave. They just want to mess with me.

Q: Hann。啊哪會你無想講若無穿，哪會知影無無佮意，穿了歹看？
Hann. Ah ná ē lí bô siūnn-kóng in nā bô tshīng, nā ē tsai-iánn bô bô kah-ì, tshīng liáu pháinn-khuànn?
Oh. But you have never thought of the possibility that they would not have known whether they like them or not, or whether the shoes look good or not if they have not tried them on?

A: 但是其實伊毋是佮意無佮意的問題。是伊，伊其實m本來就無心欲買。只是入來踅踅，<u>然後</u>看看的爾。其實，本，伊就是真的無想欲買。就是敢若有淡薄仔來亂的彼款感覺。就是無欲買按呢。
Tān-sī kî-sit i m̄ sī kah-ì bô kah-ì ê būn-tê. Sī i, i kî-sit m pún-lâi tō bô-sim beh bé. Tsí-sī jip-lâi seh-seh, <u>ran2-hou4</u> khuànn-khuànn--ê niâ. Kî-sit, pún, i tō sī tsin--ê bô siūnn beh bé. Tō sī kánn-ná ū tām-pòh-á lâi luān ê hit khuán kám-kak. Tō sī bô beh bé án-ne.
But actually this is not about whether they like it or not. It is because they, they do not wish to buy them in the first place. They only come in to walk around and take a look. Actually, they do not really want to buy. It is like they are only playing around with you. They do not want to buy.

Q: 啊人客一入來，你敢會，差不多，你一看，就差不多就知影講，這個是會買抑袂買？
Ah lâng-kheh tsit-jip--lâi, lí kám ē, tsha-put-to, lí tsit khuànn, tō tsha-put-to tsai-iánn kóng, tsit ê sī ê bé iah bē bé?
When a customer comes in, can you, approximately, can you take a look and likely know whether he will or will not buy?

A: 我無遐厲害，但是阮店的<u>小姐</u>較厲害。In一看，就知影講這个人客會買抑袂買。In感覺, in若是佇遐, 行路若按呢就是，mm足無無確定按呢, 行來行去, in就感覺講, 這个人客可能袂買矣。但是這个人客若是一入來，伊就可能行，就行佇一个所在。然後<u>直直</u>看彼排ê鞋仔。<u>然後</u>unn in就感覺講, 這人客可能是愛確定講伊伊伊欲揣啥物款的鞋仔。<u>然後</u>可能會買按呢。In較看會出來。我看無啥會出來，所以逐改攏去予人裝痟的。

Guá bô hiah lī-hāi, tān-sī guán tiàm--ê <u>xiao3-jie3</u> khah lī-hāi. In tsit khuànn, tō tsai-iánn kóng tsit ê lâng-kheh ē bé iah bē bé. In kám-kak, in nā sī tī hia, *kiânn-lōo nā án-ne tō sī, mm tsiok bô bô khak-tīng án-ne, kiânn lâi kiânn khì, in tō kám-kak kóng, tsit ê lâng-kheh khó-lîng tō bē bé--ah. Tān-sī tsit ê lâng-kheh nā sī tsit-jip--lâi, i tō khó-lîng kiânn, tō kiânn tī tsit ê sóo-tsāi. Ran2-hou4 tit-tit khuànn hit pâi ê ê-á. Ran2 -hou4 unn in tō kám-kak kóng, tsit lâng-kheh khó-lîng sī ài khak-tīng kóng i i i beh tshuē siánn-mih khuán ê ê-á. Ran2-hou4 khó-lîng ē bé án-ne. In khah khuànn ē-tshut--lâi. Guá khuànn bô siann ē-tshut--lâi, sóo-í guá tak kái lóng khì hōo lâng tsng-siáu--ê.*

I am not that good, but the ladies in our store are. They take a look, and then know instantly whether this customer will buy or not. They feel that if a customer is just standing there, if he walks this way, mm, he doesn't seem to know where he is walking to, walking back and forth, the ladies will think this person is likely not willing to buy shoes. However, if a customer comes in, and maybe immediately walks, walks to a specific section. And then he would keep on looking at the same rack of shoes. Then, um, they would feel that this customer might want to make sure what kind of shoes he he he wants to buy. Then he might buy them. The ladies are very good at doing this. I can't, so I am tricked by customers every single time.

Q: Hann。啊你的，你你欲做生理的時陣，你顧店的時陣，是對人客 hann，你講台語較濟較濟抑是國語較濟？
Hann. Ah lí ê, lí lí beh tsò-sing-lí ê sî-tsūn, lí kòo-tiàm ê sî-tsūn, sī tuì lâng-kheh hann, lí kóng Tâi-gí khah tsē khah tsē iah-sī Kok-gí khah tsē?
Hann. And your, when you you run a business, when you help in the shop, do you talk to customers in Taiwanese more or Mandarin more?

A: 講台語。因為阮阮的店是是是較近彼菜市仔，所以攏是攏是一寡媽媽啊阿婆啊。所以攏愛講台語啊。著啊。你講國語，in可能較聽無按呢。
Kóng Tâi-gí. In-uī guán guán ê tiàm sī sī sī khah kīn he tshài-tshī-á, sóo-í lóng sī lóng sī tsit-kuá má-mah--ah a-pô--ah. Sóo-í lóng ài kóng Tâi-gí--ah. Tioh--ah. Lí kóng Kok-gí, in khó-lîng khah thiann-bô án-ne.
I speak Taiwanese. Because our our shop is is is close to a local market, so customers are always moms and old ladies. So we need to speak Taiwanese. Yeah. If you speak Mandarin, they probably won't understand as much.

F4

Q: 喔 unn 請問你叫做啥物名?啊你這馬幾歲?啥物時陣出世?啊家庭的情形?啊閣有佇佗位吃頭路?啊以前佇佗位讀冊?
Ooh unn tshiánn-mñg lí kiò-tsò siánn-mih miâ? Ah lí tsit-má kuí huè? Siánn-mih sî-tsūn tshut-sì? Ah ka-tîng ê tsîng-hîng? Ah koh ū tī tó uī tsiah-thâu-lōo? Ah í-tsîng tī tó-uī thak-tsheh?

Oh, um, could you please tell me your name? And how old are you now?
When were you born? And your family? And also where do you work? And
where did you go to school?

A: 一直回答就好矣喔?
It-tit huê-tap tō hó--ah--ooh?
Do I just keep on answering?

Q: Henn henn henn.
Henn henn henn.
Yes yes yes.

A: 喔。Unn我叫做XXX。蹛佇咧台中縣太平市。以前是太平鄉啦。啊幾
年前已經升變成了,升變成了那個太平市。然後閣有啥?
*Ooh. Unn guá kiò tsò XXX. Tuà tī-leh Tâi-tiong-kuān Thài-pîng-tshī. Í-tsîng
sī Thài-pîng-hiong--lah. Ah kuí nî tsîng í-king sing bian4-cheng2-le0, sing
bian4-cheng2-le0 na4-ge0 Thài-pîng-tshī. Ran2-hou4 koh ū siánn?*
Oh. Um, my name is XXX. I live in Thài-pîng City, Tâi-tiong County. It used
to be Thài-pîng Village. But a couple of years ago, it has been upgraded and
become, upgraded and become Thài-pîng City. And then what else?

Q: 閣有啥喔?Enn你猶閣有 ...
Koh ū siánn--ooh? Enn lí iàh koh ū ...
What else? Um, you still have ...

A: 喔我今仔日,unn我今年二十四歲。Unn民國六十八年五月二十九出
生。阮兜有爸爸、媽媽、猶閣有五个姊妹仔。攏是查某的。Mm然後
佮足儕阿阿伯、阿叔、阿公、阿姆、<TECH ERR> 遮, 攏蹛佇咧彼條
街仔附近。然後我高中畢業了後, 就到台北來讀冊。然後 <TECH
ERR>間事務所做工課。然後差不多, 做差不一年, 就辭職矣。然後
繼續去一間出版社應i-應徵。然後嘛真幸運的, 會使入去做工課。猶
毋過做無偌久, 嘛差不多一年就又閣辭職矣。Mm這馬s-這馬算佇咧
厝的, 家己接khè-sù來做吧。然後 ...
*Ooh guá kin-á-jit, unn guá kin-nî jī-tsàp-sì huè. Unn Bîn-kok làk-tsàp-peh nî
gōo-guèh jī-tsàp-káu tshut-senn. Guán tau ū pá-pah, má-mah, iáu koh ū gōo ê
tsí-muē-á. Lóng sī tsa-bóo--ê. Mm ran2-hou4 kah tsiok tsē a- a-peh, a-tsik, a-
kong, a-ḿ, <TECH ERR> tsiah, lóng tuà tī-leh hit tiâu ke-á hù-kīn. Ran2-hou4
guá ko-tiong pit-giàp liáu-āu, tō kàu Tâi-pak lâi thàk-tsheh. Ran2-hou4
<TECH ERR> king sū-bū-sóo tsò khang-khuè. Ran2-hou4 tsha-put-to, tsò
tsha-put-to tsit nî, tō sî-tsit--ah. Ran2-hou4 kè-siòk khì tsit keng tshut-pán-siā
ìng i- ìng-ting. Ran2-hou4 mā tsin hīng-ūn--ê, ē-sái jip-khì tsò khang-khuè.
Iáu-ḿ-koh tsò bô-guā-kú, mā tsha-put-to tsit nî tō iū-koh sî-tsit--ah. Mm tsit-
má s- tsit-má sng tī-leh tshù--ê, ka-kī tsiap khè-sù lâi tsò pah. Ran2-hou4 ...*

Oh, today, I, unn, this year I am twenty-four years old. Um, I was born on May 29, 1979. There are Dad, Mom, and five children in my family. All are girls. Mm then we live with many uncles, grandpa, aunts, <TECH ERR> here, and we all live near that street. And after I graduated from high school, I came to Taipei to study. Then <TECH ERR> worked at an office. Then about, about one year later, I quit. Then I continued to a- apply to a publishing company. And I was really lucky and got in. However, I did not work for long, also about a year later, I quit again. Mm, now I am like a freelancer at home. And then . . .

Q: 啊閣有就是你以前佇佗位讀冊啊?
Ah koh ū tō sī lí í-tsîng tī tó-uī thàk-tsheh--ah?
Also where did you study before?

A: 我以前佇佗位讀冊?大學的時陣喔?
Guá í-tsîng tī tó-uī thàk-tsheh? Tāi-hàk ê sî-tsūn--ooh?
Where did I study before? In college?

Q: Unn.
Unn.
Uh-huh.

A: 佇咧，佇咧<u>木</u>, <u>木柵</u>的<u>政治大學</u>啊。讀<u>日文系</u>喔。因為以前對日本就足有興趣的，所以高中畢業了後，就，<u>填志願的時候</u>，就<u>直接填日文系矣</u>。
Tī-leh, tī-leh <u>Mu4</u>, <u>Mu4-zha4</u> ê <u>Zheng4-zhi4-da4-xue2</u>--ah. Thàk <u>Ri4-wen2-xi4</u>--ooh. In-uī í-tsîng tuì Jit-bûn tō tsiok ū hìng-tshù--ê, sóo-í ko-tiong pit-giàp liáu-āu, tō, <u>tian2 zhi4-yuan4 de0 shi2-hou4</u>, tō <u>zhi2-jie1 tian2 Ri4-wen2-xi4</u>--ah.
At Chengchi University in Mu, Muzha. I studied Japanese. Because I used to be very interested in Japanese, when I was applying for college after high school graduation, I immediately chose Japanese.

Q: 喔。你是毋是無啥習慣佮我講台語?
Ooh. Lí sī m̄ sī bô siánn sip-kuàn kap guá kóng Tâi-gí?
Oh. Are you not used to talking to me in Taiwanese?

A: 有一寡。S- enn unn按呢講較無自然啦。佇咧厝講就真gâu講啊。
Ū tsit-kuá. S- enn unn án-ne kóng khah bô tsū-jiân--lah. Tī-leh tshù kóng tō tsin gâu kóng--ah.
A little bit. S- um um to talk in this way is not that natural. When I am at home I am very good at speaking Taiwanese.

Q: 喔。
Ooh.
Oh.

References

Ang, U. (1992). *Taiwan Fangyan zhi Lyu [The Journey of Taiwan Vernacular]*. Avanguard.

Ang, U. (1997). *Kaohsiungxian Minnanyu Fangyan [Southern Min Dialects in Kaohsiung County]*. Kaohsiung County Government.

Ang, U. (2003). The Motivation and Direction of Sound Change: On the Competition of Minnan Dialects Chang-chou and Chuan-chou and the Emergence of General Taiwanese [PhD]. National Tsing Hua University.

Ang, U. (2012). The drift of change of the initial /j-/ of Southern Min. *Journal of Taiwanese Languages and Literature*, 7(2), 1–32.

Balise, R. R. & Diehl, R. L. (1994). Some distributional facts about fricatives and a perceptual explanation. *Phonetica: International Journal of Speech Science*, *51*(1–3), 99–110.

Chang, C.-H. (1989). *Taiwan Minnan Fangyan Jilue [Notes on Southern Min Dialects]*. Liberal Arts Press.

Chang, P.-S. (1999). *Xianxing Taiwanhuazhong de Riyu Cihui Gao [A Manuscript on the Japanese Vocabulary in Current Taiwanese]*.

Chang, P.-S. (2000). *Taiwan Minnanyu Bufen Cifangyan de Yuyin he Cihui Chayi [Differences in Phonemes and Vocabulary in Some Subdialects of Taiwan Southern Min]*. National Pingtung University.

Chao, Y. R. (1956). Tone, intonation, singsong, chanting, recitative, tonal composition, and atonal composition in Chinese. In M. Halle (ed.), *For Roman Jakobson* (pp. 52–59). Mouton.

Chao, Y. R. (1968). *A Grammar of Spoken Chinese*. University of California Press.

Chappell, H. (2019). Southern Min. In A. Vittrant & J. Watkins (eds.), *The Mainland Southeast Asia Linguistic Area* (pp. 176–233). De Gruyter.

Chen G.-Y. (1998). *Wenhua, Yilan, Youxikun [Culture, Yilan, Si-Kun You]*. Yuan-Liou.

Chen, M. Y. (1987). The syntax of Xiamen tone sandhi. *Phonology*, *4*, 109–149.

Chen, P.-Y. (2021). An Acoustic Approach to the Tone Variations of Quanzhou Accent in Taiwan's Southern Min: A Case Study of Wuqi Town, Taichung City [MA]. National Kaohsiung Normal University.

Chen, S.-C. (1995). Guanmiao Fangyan "Chu-gui-shi" de Yanjiu [A Study on the Sound Change from the Chu-Rhyme to the Shi-Rhyme in Guanmiao Dialect] [MA]. National Taiwan University.

Chen S.-C. (2004). Phonological Change and Language Shift of Taiwanese Hokkien in *Toa-gu-tiau*, Taoyuen [PhD]. National Taiwan University.

Chen, S.-C. (2009a). Tainanshi fangyan de yuyin bianyi yu bianhua [Sound variation and sound change in Tainan City]. *Bulletin of Chinese Phonology, 16*, 137–175.

Chen, S.-C. (2009b). The vowel system change and the Yin-/Yang-entering tonal variations in Taiwanese Hokkien. *Journal of Taiwanese Language and Literature, 3*, 157–178.

Chen, S.-C. (2010a). Multilingualism in Taiwan. *International Journal of the Sociology of Language, 2010*(205), 79–104.

Chen, S.-C. (2010b). New sound variation in Taiwan Southern Min: Vowel systems and the lower register entering tone in Taipei, Changhua, and Tainan. *Language and Linguistics Compass, 11*(2), 425–468.

Chen, S.-C. (2013). The sound variation and change of Shezi dialect in Taipei City. *Language and Linguistics, 14*(2), 371–408.

Chen, S.-C. (2014). Sound variation and change in the dialect of Guishan Island. *Bulletin of the Department of Chinese Literature, 21*, 213–243.

Chen, S.-C. (2017). Sound variations and changes in Taiwanese Hokkien dialect in northern and southern Yi-lan. *Journal of Taiwanese Languages and Literature, 12*(2), 187–215.

Chen, S.-C. (2018). Dialect borrowing or natural change: Sound change and variation in old Tongan-based Southern Min of Hsinchu. *Bulletin of Chinese, 64*, 251–285.

Chen, S.-C. (2021). The differences between Changchou and Chuanchou accents as well as new sound variations of Taiwanese Hokkien in Tatu, Taichung. *Tunghai Journal of Chinese Literature, 42*, 105–143.

Chen, S.-C. & Chen, Y.-C. (2020). A study of sound variation and sound change in the Taiwanese Southern Min of Hualien: A survey of three varieties – Hualien City, Juisui and Fuli. *Journal of Taiwanese Languages and Literature, 15*(2), 157–206.

Cheng, R. L. (1973). Some notes on tone sandhi in Taiwanese. *Linguistics and Philosophy, 100*, 5–25.

Cheng, R. L. & Cheng, S. S. (1987). *Phonological Structure and Romanization of Taiwanese Hokkian*. Student Book.

Chiang, W.-Y. (1992). The Prosodic Morphology and Phonology of Affixation in Taiwanese and Other Chinese Languages [PhD]. University of Delaware. www.proquest.com/dissertations-theses/prosodic-morphology-phonology-affixation/docview/303970491/se-2.

Chiung, W.-V. (2002). *Tâi-gí ê bí /bi/ hâm Ing-gí ê "bee" kám ū-iánn kāng-khuán? – Uì voice onset time ê kuan-tiám khuànn Tâi-gí hâm Ing-gí ê that-in ê tsha-ī [Is "Rice" /bi/ in Taiwanese Really the Same as "Bee" in English? – Looking at the Differences in Stops between Taiwanese and English from the*

Viewpoint of Voice Onset Time]. The 4th International Symposium on Taiwanese Languages and Teaching, Kaohsiung.

Chou, W.-Y. (1996). The Kōminka Movement in Taiwan and Korea: Comparisons and interpretations. In P. Duus, R. H. Myers & M. R. Peattie (eds.), *The Japanese Wartime Empire, 1931–1945* (pp. 40–68). Princeton University Press.

Chuang, Y.-Y. & Fon, J. (2017a). On the dialectal variations of voiced sibilant /dz/ in Taiwan Min young speakers. *Lingua Sinica, 3*(1). https://doi.org/10.1186/s40655-016-0016-x.

Chuang, Y.-Y. & Fon, J. (2017b). *The Effect of Visual Talker Information on the Perception and Representation of Phonetic Variations in Taiwan Mandarin.* 11th International Conference on Cognitive Science, Taipei, Taiwan.

Chuang, Y.-Y. & Fon, J. (2018). The effect of speaker gender and talker proficiency on the realization of Taiwan Min /dz/ among young speakers. *Lingua Sinica, 4*(1). https://linguasinica.springeropen.com/articles/10.1186/s40655-017-0033-4.

Chu, M.-N. & Lin, H.-W. (2010). Coda discrimination is governed by acoustic and phonological constraints: A case study of the generalized linear model. *Tsing Hua Journal of Chinese Studies, 40*(1), 47–66.

Chung, R.-F. (1996). *The Segmental Phonology of Southern Min in Taiwan.* Crane.

Clements, G., Vaissière, J., Amelot, A. & Montagu, J. (2015). The feature [nasal]. In A. Rialland, R. Ridouane & H. van der Hulst (eds.), *Features in Phonology and Phonetics: Posthumous Writings by Nick Clements and Coauthors* (pp. 195–215). De Gruyter Mouton.

Dai, L. (2007). The phonology of the Putian dialect as found in the local Chinese version of the New Testament and Psalms (1912). *Zhongguo Yuwen, 2007*(1), 35–45.

Fon, J. (2004). *A Preliminary Construction of Taiwan Southern Min Spontaneous Speech Corpus* (NSC-92-2411-H-003-050-). National Science Council.

Fon, J. & Chiang, W.-Y. (1999). What does Chao have to say about tones? A case study of Taiwan Mandarin. *Journal of Chinese Linguistics, 27*(1), 15–37.

Fon, J., Chiang, W.-Y. & Cheung, H. (2004). Production and perception of two dipping tones (T2 and T3) in Taiwan Mandarin. *Journal of Chinese Linguistics, 32*(2), 249–280.

Gandour, J. (1977). On the interaction between tone and vowel length: Evidence from Thai dialects. *Phonetica: International Journal of Speech Science, 34*, 54–65.

Hayashi, W., Hsu, C.-S. & Keating, P. (1999). Domain-initial strengthening in Taiwanese: A follow-up study. *UCLA Working Papers in Phonetics, 97*, 152–156.

Hong, S.-W. & Chan, R. W. (2022). Acoustic analysis of Taiwanese tones in esophageal speech and pneumatic artificial laryngeal speech. *Journal of Speech, Language, and Hearing Research, 65*(4), 1215–1227.

Howie, J. M. (1974). On the domain of tone in Mandarin. *Phonetica: International Journal of Speech Science, 30*, 129–148.

Hsieh, W.-C. (2007). The Acoustic Study on the Phonetic System of Southern Min [MA]. National Kaohsiung Normal University.

Hsu, C.-S. & Jun, S.-A. (1996). Is tone sandhi group part of the prosodic hierarchy in Taiwanese? *Journal of the Acoustical Society of America, 100* (4_Supplement), 2824.

Hsu, C.-S. K. & Jun, S. A. (1998). Prosodic strengthening in Taiwanese: Syntagmatic or paradigmatic? *UCLA Working Papers in Phonetics, 96,* 69–89.

Hsu, H.-C. (2004). Compositional structure of /iu/ and /ui/ in Taiwanese Southern Min revisited. *Language and Linguistics Compass, 5*(4), 1003–1018.

Hsu, H.-J. (2015). Taro or oyster? The production merger of the two mid back vowels, [o] and [ɔ], in a major dialect of Taiwan Southern Min. *Dialectologia et Geolinguistica, 23*(1), 68–94.

Hsu, H.-J. (2016). Biandongzhong de Taiyu: Taiyu /o/ yinsu sanzhong zhuyao duyin de xianzhuang fenxi [Taiwanese in transition: An analysis of the current status of the three main pronunciations of the Taiwanese phoneme /o/]. *Soochow Journal of Chinese Studies, 31*, 303–328.

Hsu, H.-J. (2018). The entanglement of emotion and reality: An investigation of the Taiwanese people's attitudes towards Taigi. *Journal of Multilingual and Multicultural Development, 39*(1), 76–91.

Huang, S. (1993). *Yuyan, Shehui yu Zuqun Yishi: Taiwan yuyan shehuixue de yanjiu [Language, Society, and Ethnic Identity: Studies in Language Sociology in Taiwan].* Crane.

Huang, S.-S. (2009). Taiwan Minnango gotō haretsuon no VOT zuhi bunpu: Taipei chiku ni okeru shirabe chōcha [The distribution of VOT values of word-initial plosives in Taiwanese Southern Min: A survey on the Taipei area]. *Kōpasu Ni Motodzuku Gengogaku Kyōiku Kenkyū Hōkoku [Research Reports on Corpus-Based Linguistics and Language Education], 2,* 105–115.

Ichikawa, H. (2013). A study of editing teaching materials of Taiwanese Hō-ló-uē under early Japanese ruled period: Concerning Japanese cognition and understanding to Hō-ló-uē. *Monumenta Taiwanica, 8,* 29–58.

Jongman, A., Qin, Z., Zhang, J. & Sereno, J. A. (2017). Just noticeable differences for pitch direction, height, and slope for Mandarin and English listeners. *Journal of the Acoustical Society of America, 142*(2), EL163–EL169.

Jun, S.-A. (ed.). (2005). *Prosodic Typology: The Phonology of Intonation and Phrasing.* Oxford University Press.

Kendall, T. & Thomas, E. R. (2018). *Vowels: Vowel Manipulation, Normalization, and Plotting.* https://CRAN.R-project.org/package=vowels.

Khng, S.-T. (2014). A Phonetic Survey and Variation Analysis of Taiwanese in Kaohsiung [MA]. National Taiwan Normal University.

Khoo, H.-L. (2019). The dynamics of Southern Min in Taiwan: From Southern Min dialects to "Taigi." In C. Shei (ed.), *The Routledge Handbook of Chinese Discourse Analysis* (pp. 596–610). Routledge.

Kuo, G. (2011). Prosodic boundaries and the Taiwanese tone sandhi group. *UCLA Working Papers in Phonetics, 109,* 40–59.

Kuo, G. (2012). Perceived prosodic boundaries in Taiwanese and their acoustic correlates. *Proceedings of Interspeech 2012,* 1953–1956.

Labov, W. (2001). *Principles of Linguistic Change, vol. 2: Social Factors.* Blackwell.

Li, Y.-S. & Myers, J. (2005). Modeling variation in Taiwan Southern Min syllable contraction. *Taiwan Journal of Linguistics, 3*(2), 79–118.

Lien, C. (1995). Taiwan Minnanyu cizhui "a" de yanjiu [A study on the suffix -a in Taiwan Southern Min]. *Proceedings of the Second International Symposium on Languages in Taiwan,* 465–483.

Lin, C.-H. (2001). *Taiwan Minnanyu Gailun [An Introduction to Taiwan Southern Min].* Psychological.

Lin, J.-T. (1995). Taiwan Minnanyu sandai jian yuyin cihui de chubu diaocha yu bijiao: Yi Kaohsiung Xiaogang weili [A Preliminary Investigation on the Phonetics of Some Lexical Items Comparing Across Three Generations of Taiwan Min Speakers: Using the Lin Family in Xiaogang, Kaohsiung City as an Example] [MA]. National Taiwan Normal University.

Lin, M. C.-Y. (2013). *A Study of the Production and Perception of Aspirated and Unaspirated Stops in Taiwan Mandarin and Taiwan Southern Min* (K.-P. Tse, ed.) [MA]. National Taiwan Normal University.

Lin, Y.-C. (2021). Zhanhou chuqi Taiwan tuixing Guoyuyundong zhi tantao: 1945–1949 [Taiwan's Mandarin promotion movement in the early postwar period: 1945–1949]. *Journal of Science and Technology and Humanities of Transworld Institute, 27,* 19–31.

Liu K.-M. (2010). *Taiwan Jingu Tan [About Taiwan Then and Now].* Cheng Wen.

Lobanov, B. M. (1971). Classification of Russian vowels spoken by different listeners. *Journal of the Acoustic Society of America, 49,* 606–608.

Lu, K.-C. (2003). *Taiwan Minnanyu Gaiyao [An Introduction to Taiwan Southern Min].* Southern Material Center.

Ministry of Culture ROC (2019). Development of National Languages Act. Laws and Regulations Database of the Republic of China (Taiwan). https://law.moj.gov.tw/ENG/LawClass/LawAll.aspx?pcode=H0170143.

Ministry of Education ROC (2008). *Taiwan Minnanyu Luomazi Pinyin Fangan shiyong shouce [A User's Manual on the Taiwanese Southern Min Romanization Spelling Scheme]*. https://ws.moe.edu.tw/001/Upload/FileUpload/3677-15601/Documents/tshiutsheh.pdf.

Ministry of Education ROC (2014). *Taiwan Minnanyu tuijian yongzi 700 zibiao [Recommended Character List of 700 Words for Taiwan Southern Min]*. https://ws.moe.edu.tw/001/Upload/userfiles/file/iongji/700iongji_1031222.pdf.

Ministry of Education ROC (2020). *Taiwan Minnanyu Changyongci Cidian [Dictionary of Frequent Words in Taiwanese Southern Min]*. Ministry of Education ROC.

National Statistics ROC (2021). *109 nian renkou ji zhuzhai pucha zongbaogao tiyao fenxi [The 2020 Population and Housing Census: A General Summary Report on the Statistic Results and Analyses]*. www.stat.gov.tw/News.aspx?n=2750&sms=11062.

Ogawa, N. (1907). *Nittai Dai Jiten [A Composite Japanese-Taiwanese Dictionary]*. Formosa Governor Office.

Ogawa, N. (1931). *Tai-Nichi Daijiten [A Composite Taiwanese-Japanese Dictionary, vol. 1]*. Formosa Governor Office.

Ogawa, N. (1932). *Tai-Nichi Daijiten [A Composite Taiwanese-Japanese Dictionary, vol. 2]*. Formosa Governor Office.

Ohala, J. J. (1983). The origin of sound patterns in vocal tract constraints. In P. F. MacNeilage (ed.), *The Production of Speech* (pp. 189–216). Springer.

Pan, H.-H. (1995). *The Phonetic Variants of Taiwanese "Voiced" Stops: An Airflow Study*.

Pan, H.-H. (2004). Nasality in Taiwanese. *Language and Speech, 47*(3), 267–296.

Pan, H.-H. (2007a). Focus and Taiwanese unchecked tones. In C. Lee, M. Gordon & D. Büring (eds.), *Topic and Focus: Cross-linguistic Perspectives on Meaning and Intonation, vol. 82* (pp. 195–213). Springer.

Pan, H.-H. (2007b). Initial strengthening of lexical tones in Taiwanese Min. In C. Gussenhoven & T. Riad (eds.), *Tones and Tunes Volume 2: Experimental Studies in Word and Sentence Prosody* (pp. 271–292). De Gruyter.

Pan, H.-H. (2007c). The effects of prosodic boundaries on nasality in Taiwan Min. *Journal of the Acoustical Society of America, 121*(6), 3755–3769.

Pan, H.-H. (2017). Glottalization of Taiwan Min checked tones. *Journal of the International Phonetic Association, 47*(1), 37–63.

Pan, H.-H. & Lyu, S. R. (2021). Taiwan Min Nan (Taiwanese) checked tones sound change. *22nd Annual Conference of the International Speech Communication Association, INTERSPEECH 2021*, 1818–1822.

Pan, H.-H., Lyu, S.-R., Huang, H.-T. & Mu-fan, W. (2018). Taiwanese Min juncture tones and prosodic boundaries. *Proceedings of the Sixth International Symposium on Tonal Aspects of Languages*, 37–40.

Pan, H.-H. & Tai, Y.-H. (2006). Boundaries and tonal articulation in Taiwanese Min. *Proceedings of Speech Prosody*, Paper 134.

Peng, S.-H. (1997). Production and perception of Taiwanese tones in different tonal and prosodic contexts. *Journal of Phonetics*, *25*(3), 371–400.

Peng, S.-H. & Beckman, E. M. (2003). Annotation conventions and corpus design in the investigation of spontaneous speech prosody in Taiwanese. *Proceedings of the ISCA & IEEE Workshop on Spontaneous Speech Processing and Recognition*, 17–22.

Peng, S.-H., Chan, M. K. M., Tseng, C.-Y., Huang, T., Lee, O. J. & Beckman, E. M. (2005). Towards a pan-Mandarin system for prosodic transcription. In S.-A. Jun (ed.), *Prosodic Typology: The Phonology of Intonation and Phrasing* (pp. 230–270). Oxford University Press.

Pierrehumbert, J. (1980). *The Phonology and Phonetics of English Intonation* [PhD]. Massachusetts Institute of Technology.

R Core Team. (2021). *R: A Language and Environment for Statistical Computing*. R Foundation for Statistical Computing, Vienna, Austria. www.R-project.org.

Selkirk, E. (1986). On derived domains in sentence phonology. *Phonology*, *3*, 371–405.

Shi, F. & Wang, P. (2006). A statistic analysis of the tones in Beijing Mandarin. *Studies of the Chinese Language*, *1*, 33–40.

Shih, C.-L. (1988). Tone and intonation in Mandarin. *Working Papers of the Cornell Phonetics Laboratory*, *3*, 83–109.

Ting, P.-H. (1985). *Taiwan Yuyan Yuanliu (Sources of Languages in Taiwan)*. Student Book.

Tiu^n, J. (2009). *TJ's Dictionary of Non-literary Taiwanese*. Asian A-tsiu International.

Tseng, C.-H. & Huang, K.-Y. (1992). Taiwanhua seyin qingzhuodu de shengxue guance: VOT de chubu fenxu baogao [Acoustic observations of voiced and voiceless stops in Taiwanese: A preliminary analysis on VOT]. *Journal of the Speech-Language-Hearing Association*, *8*, 2–12.

Tung, C.-H. (1968). *The Phonological System of Gaoxiong, a Min Dialect of Chinese, vol. 5.2*. University of California Press.

Tung, C.-S. (1991). Taibeishi, Tainanshi, Lugang, Yilan fangyan yinxi de zhengli han bijiao [A cross-dialectal compilation and comparison of the phonological systems in Taipei City, Tainan City, Lugang, and Ilan]. *Journal of National Hsin Chu Teachers College, 5*, 31–64.

Tu, W.-C. (2011). The types and districts of Min-Nan dialect in Changhua County. *Journal of Taiwanese Language and Literature, 6*(2), 111–145.

Tung C.-S. (1996). *Taiwan Minnanyu Yuyin Jiaocai Chugao [A Preliminary Manuscript on the Teaching Materials for Taiwan Southern Min Phonetics].* Council for Cultural Affairs, ROC.

Tung, C.-S. (2001). *Fuermosha de Laoyin: Taiwan Minnanyu gaiyao [Branding of Formosa: An introduction to Taiwan Southern Min].* Council for Cultural Affairs, Executive Yuan, ROC.

Wang, H. S. (1996). A concept formation experiment for Taiwan Min voiced stop consonants. *International Symposium on Chinese Languages and Linguistics,* 320–329.

Wang, H.-W. (2014). The Performances of the Kinmen Dialect of Young People in Kinmen Using 8 Young People Born in Kinmen in the 80s as Examples [MA]. National Taiwan Normal University.

Wong, W. Y. P., Chan, M. K. M. & Beckman, M. E. (2005). An autosegmental-metrical analysis and prosodic annotation conventions for Cantonese. In S.-A. Jun (ed.), *Prosodic Typology: The Phonology of Intonation and Phrasing* (pp. 271–300). Oxford University Press.

Wu, M.-C. (2000). *Taiwanshi Xiaoshidian [A Concise Dictionary of the Events in Taiwan History].* Yuan-Liou.

Yang, H.-F. (1988). *Tainanshizhi Renminzhi Yuyanpian.* Tainan City Government.

Yang, H.-F. (1991). *Taiwan Minnanyu Yufa Gao [A Manuscript on the Grammar of Taiwanese Southern Min].* Ta-an Press.

Yap, K.-H. (2018). A review of linguistic surveys in censuses of Taiwan. *Journal of Taiwanese Languages and Literature, 13*(2), 247–274.

Yu, A. C. L. (2010). Tonal effects on perceived vowel duration. In C. Fougeron, B. Kühnert, M. D'Imperio & N. Vallée (eds.), *Laboratory Phonology 10* (pp. 151–168). Walter de Gruyter.

Printed by Integrated Books International,
United States of America